GOING INTO BUSINESS
HOW TO DO IT, BY THE MAN WHO DID IT

GOING INTO BUSINESS
HOW TO DO IT, BY THE MAN WHO DID IT

Eugene Ferkauf
Founder of E.J. KORVETTE

CHELSEA HOUSE PUBLISHERS
New York, London
1977

This book would never have been started or completed without the assistance of my wife, Estelle, and the efforts of the entire staff of Penfield Retail Services, Inc. and Penfield Publishing Company, Inc., especially Lou Wachtel, Joe Zwillenberg, Irwin Hochberg and Elayne Beloten.

Eugene Ferkauf

Project Editor: **Karyn Gullen Browne**
Managing Editor: **Laurie Likoff**
Art Director: **Susan Lusk**

Library of Congress Cataloging in Publication Data

Ferkauf, Eugene, 1920-
  Going into business.

  1. Retail trade—Handbooks, manuals, etc.
2. Korvettes—History. I. Title.
HF5429.F37   658.8'7   77-3395
ISBN 0-87754-049-7

CHELSEA HOUSE PUBLISHERS

Harold Steinberg, Chairman & Publisher   Andrew E. Norman, President
A Division of Chelsea House Educational Communications, Inc.
70 West 40th Street, New York, N.Y. 10018

For Howard Kleinberg, Howard Bronstein, Joshua Kleinberg, Ronald Bronstein and Daniel Shapira.

Contents

Retailing in the Years Ahead

The Story of E.J. Korvette

1

How I Started E.J. Korvette

E. J. KORVETTE, AND ALL THAT THE NAME HAS COME TO REPRESENT in retailing, began in a modest way with my father's luggage business in New York City. He had two shops, the Terminal Luggage Store on Fifth Avenue and Rex Luggage on Lexington Avenue. Before the Second World War, he ran the shop on Lexington himself, but when I returned from the service, I took over for him there and he went to Fifth Avenue.

My father, Harry Ferkauf, was quite successful in the luggage industry. I think it would be safe to say that he was one of the most successful luggage retailers in the United States, and when I assumed charge of the Lexington shop, it was easy for me to see why he had done so well. This store was so well organized that it was extremely easy to operate. Since it also occupied a splendid location on a busy avenue, it made a great deal of money. We always had plenty of money in the bank because we paid our bills on the same day merchandise was received. Consequently, our accounts payable were customarily near zero.

Nevertheless, my father and I had philosophical differences about how to run the store. He was a traditionalist. Coming from Romania to America as a child, he had traveled the familiar immigrant road, establishing his original business as a manufacturer of commercial leather goods. The Depression precipitated him into retailing, and in 1931 he opened his store on Lexington Avenue. It was a distant cry from what he had hoped to be as a young man. His entire family were theatre people, and as they expected, he had become an actor. But on the day I was born, he quit acting and took his new responsibility as a father with the utmost seriousness. He never got the theatre out of his blood and remained a patron of the arts all his life. He enjoyed sports as well. The only thing he really hated was business and he tried to discourage me from going into it.

I was born in Manhattan, November 13, 1920, but I grew up in Brooklyn. My educational background was the usual time spent at P.S. 219 in East Flatbush, and then on to Samuel Tilden High School, where Sam Levinson, the humorist and author, at one time taught Spanish. In 1937, at the age of 16, I attended City College at night to study accounting but quit school after one semester.

During my teens, my father's major effort to steer me away from business was to finance my study of the piano. I had no more patience with it than I did with formal education. My whole instinct was toward the business world my father despised, and reluctantly he gave in. On the day of my graduation from high school he presented me with the keys to the Lexington Avenue store.

I worked six days a week full-time in the beautiful Rex Luggage store, but I was still under my father's wing. The time I spent in charge there was a far cry from the messenger work, saddle-soaping and occasional selling I had done previously for my father while I was still in high school.

As I didn't seem to want anything more, I continued the operation of the store as run by my father until I enlisted in the Army in 1942 at age 22. Before going on a tour overseas to the Philippines and Tokyo, I met my wife, the former Estelle Silverstein, while canoeing in Prospect Park in Brooklyn. We were married in June, 1945, shortly before I left for the Philippines.

The keys to the Rex Luggage store were returned to my father for the duration of my Army tour. This was intended to be a temporary measure only, but it became a permanent situation when I returned from the war after more than 43 months. I was like a tiger looking for prey—anxious for action and thirsting for large events. With a retail operation again at my disposal, I focused all my energy and thought into converting a traditional luggage store into a discount shop. This was not an original idea by any means. About the turn of the century, a man named Charles W. Wolf had operated a retail luggage shop on lower Broadway near the financial district. Besides running his store in the usual manner of retail selling, Wolf visited the purchasing departments of the major corporations nearby and wrote huge orders for briefcases and all kinds of commercial leather goods. One day he conceived the idea of leaving a batch of identifying discount cards for the personnel in these firms, so that he could service the rank-and-file as well as the executives. An employee, bearing one of these cards, could come to his store and by showing it, get a 25 percent discount on his purchases.

Merchandise that came into Wolf's store was marked up 10 percent initially to cover the overhead—then the price was doubled. Thus, a leather attaché case that cost Wolf $10, was marked up to $11 and sold at $22 to anyone who came in off the street and bought it. But if a customer had one of the discount cards that Wolf left with the big corporations, he or she could buy the case for $16.50. That, as far as I know, was the beginning of discounting.

Wolf subsequently died after a fall from a horse, but he had been highly successful in his time and was an example for others. About six other stores took their cue from him and operating in the same fashion, made large fortunes. Even in the mid-thirties, when the country was still struggling to get back on its feet financially, these few aggressive retailers were incredibly successful, while the others who were still operating in the conventional way continued to have a hard time.

Other types of retailers were also discovering the advantages of discounting. Catalog stores were a prime example, although they got into discounting through the back door. These stores originated with the small retail shops, usually on the second floor of office buildings or in low-rent areas, and occupied no more than 2,000 square feet. They were really jewelry stores and that was how they made their money. In order to establish themselves more firmly as legitimate businesses and in an effort to attract more customers, they originated the catalog, which listed famous brands of merchandise offered at discount prices. Merchandise sold from the catalog was not important to them at first; what they wanted was jewelry customers. They prospered during the thirties and forties and are back on the scene again today, but somewhere along the way, the original stores made serious mistakes and many of them have failed.

But I had neither a catalog store nor a jewelry store on Lexington Avenue. I had a luggage store, and I was blessed with a father who subordinated his ambitions to those of my own. Though he was a successful man, a rich man, his mind wasn't preoccupied with making money. He wanted me to spend my time going to museums, to the theatre and to good movies. I respected him and understood what he was trying to do for me, but I resisted his efforts to push me towards the arts. Again, I think my resistance was understandable. It was 1947 and I'd just come back from the war; I was married and had a baby girl, Barbara. I was filled with a tremendous sense of initiative, charged inside with a kind of driving force, and I was looking for somewhere to direct all of this energy.

In short, I had it made in the Lexington Avenue store, but I had made up my mind to start a retail business of my own, specifically a discount luggage store, of the same kind that I'd been trying to create for my father. It took some courage to make the break. I had valuable experience as an asset, but financially I had only $4,000 with which to begin a new business and I made no attempt to get extra capital. As I wandered the streets looking for a possible location, I began for the first time to have anxieties about whether I could swing it.

One day during the lunch hour in the Spring of 1948, while sitting on one of the marble benches in the Rockefeller Center Promenade at Radio City watching the people stream past, I gave myself a short lecture. I hadn't told my father what I intended to do, but I told myself not to be frightened. I would take my courage in hand and go into business for myself. The water might be icy, but I had to plunge in no matter what happened.

Within a week, I once again returned the Lexington Avenue store keys to my father. I knew it was a blow to him, but I never knew until after his death one year later at age 54 of a heart attack, that he had quietly okayed the accounts I opened with vendors for my new store. After his death, the store was run by my mother, Rose, and my sister, Lauretta, until the building was demolished to make way for an inevitable skyscraper. My mother by this time had no lease on the store, but the landlord, Joseph Kennedy, generously compensated them for the loss of the business.

I would have preferred a ground-floor location for my new business, but I simply couldn't afford the rent and had to settle for the second floor of a small, rather old and dingy office building on Forty-sixth Street between Fifth and Madison avenues. Despite its condition, it was in an excellent location—the heart of the Grand Central Station area, which in 1948, was the very best part of the city.

I had a name picked out for the store, E. J. Korvette. In spite of the colorful stories about its origin, the truth is more prosaic, but for me, more meaningful. "E" is for Eugene, my first name, and "J" stands for Joe Zwillenberg, my associate and my pal. Joe had been my closest friend since boyhood; without him I never could have finished my math homework. We grew up together in Brooklyn. Joe went to Brooklyn College, where he was a boxing champion, and three months after graduation found himself in the Army. We served together in the Philippines and met after he came off Corregidor. While we were sitting in Rizal Stadium watching a baseball game, we began discussing going into business together, and out of that conversation came our association in the new store that I opened in June, 1948.

As for "Korvette," it was originally meant to be spelled with a "C" after the Canadian marine sub-destroyer, simply because I thought the name had a euphonious ring. When it came time to register the name, we found it was illegal to use a naval class identity, so we had to change the spelling to "K." There's no more mystery to the store's name than what I've set down here, in spite of the tales about "eight Jewish Korean War veterans" and other variations you may hear.

Despite starting a business with only $4,000, I soon acquired valuable assets in the form of the young men I hired. Murray Beilenson was my first employee. I was lucky to get Murray, who, until recently, stayed with the E. J. Korvette chain. Someone had recommended him to me, and like so many other things that happened, it was a stroke of good fortune.

"I'm going to start a business," I told him. "Would you like to join me?"

Murray agreed. He never even asked me how much I was going to pay him—he simply quit his job and joined me, and from the day he started he was a tremendous help. He had four years of experience in the Army Quartermaster Corps, so that when it came to handling merchandise, Murray knew most of what there was to know about it.

Together, Murray and I opened the store at 6 East Forty-sixth Street, approximately 400 square feet on the second floor. All the merchandise had to be carried up the steps.

To help stimulate business, we presented discount cards to large firms operating in the Grand Central Station area, and offered one-third off on name-brand, fair-traded merchandise. I picked the names of the firms out of a telephone book and went to visit them myself: Texaco, the Girl Scouts, the New York Central Railroad, American Oil, the United Nations. The only advertising done to announce the opening of the store was to distribute the discount cards and to place fact sheets, showing the discounted prices, on bulletin boards of companies in the area.

Although I dealt mainly with the same suppliers and manufacturers used by my father's store, I shortened the markup on all items, so that all could be sold at a 33⅓ percent discount. We dealt with three types of goods: small appliances (such as steam irons, food mixers and manual juicers), jewelry (such as pins, Ronson lighters, Remington shavers and travel clocks) and luggage. Since the 33⅓ percent discount represented my exact wholesale price for the appliances and jewelry, I was prepared initially to make no profit on any of the merchandise sold except luggage and leather goods.

We were unbelievably busy from the opening day. I had thought that the beginning would be slow and gentle, that we would have to persuade customers in more than the ordinary ways, so I had a bar set up to serve them when they climbed the stairs to shop. The idea was that when a person came up to buy an attaché case, for instance, we would offer him or her a drink, after the sale was made. I thought it would be that kind of easygoing affair. My chief worry was whether people would climb up to the second floor of a dilapidated building.

I needn't have worried. We were jammed from the day we started. In the first week of operation we sold out the last piece of merchandise. To keep operating from day to day, I had to bring my car into the city, go to A. Cohen & Sons distributors, fill my car in the morning and bring merchandise to the store so that we would have something to sell.

To accommodate the huge number of customers each day, we were faced with the operational problem of how to keep stock on the shelves. We carried many brands and often substituted one name brand for another at the same price. In the first, second and third years of operation, we turned over our inventories 33 times each year. This meant everyone who worked for us had to have a strong back because we had incoming deliveries all day, every day, and the heavy merchandise as well as the light had to be carried up a flight of stairs. A few customers pitched in and helped us carry the goods so they could get their merchandise.

Before the end of 1948 we had four employees: myself, Murray Beilenson, Joe Zwillenberg, my friend and accounting genius, and George Yelen, who eventually became chairman of the board of E. J. Korvette. However, it was not unusual to see my wife, Estelle, and her sister, Florence, helping in ways that were too valuable to ever account.

With only four people working in the store, we did approximately $1 million in sales volume in the first year, all out of a space of 400 square feet. We had no warehouse, no storage area, none of the usual commercial amenities. During our first Christmas season, in which we averaged $13,000 in sales a day, we had to shut the doors at 6 p.m.— then work half the night getting things ready for the next day. We slept briefly in a nearby hotel and were back to work at 8 o'clock in the morning—often finding a line of people that stretched around the block waiting to get into the store.

Those first weeks and months of carrying merchandise up the stairs taught us at least one lesson. Later, in future E. J. Korvette stores, we built sidewalk chutes to get the goods into the basement, sometimes with unexpected results. One of our buyers in the Forty-second Street store was once waiting at the bottom of the chute for merchandise to slide down, when a woman came hurtling into his arms. She had been walking by and had inadvertently stepped into an unprotected chute opening. By reflex action he reached out and said, "Who the hell ordered this?" History doesn't record what the woman said. We were thankful she didn't sue us. Some employees, on hearing about this incident, discovered a way to do themselves some good. If they were late for work, on occasion they would slide down a chute, shed their coats, and walk casually upstairs as though they had been at work all the time.

Looking back at our beginnings on Forty-sixth Street, I can scarcely believe how we managed, particularly without any receiving facilities. In the following years, whenever I signed a lease I made sure that it was possible to get merchandise onto the premises easily.

I learned a great deal as we went along. To begin with, our original concept was that of a fine luggage store and any other items were to be an accommodation. During our first year, we bought a tremendous tonnage of merchandise in the "accommodation" category. Nearly every salesperson of small appliances and better housewares in the city was putting his head through our door each day, knowing he would get an order.

A system of ordering goods had to be worked out because we were hard-pressed between receiving merchandise and waiting on the customers. We were always working on the floor, and when a salesperson appeared in the doorway, we called out to him whatever the last 15-minute shortage happened to be. We would bellow, "Send in 96 of this, or 144 of that and get the hell out of here." That, without any exaggeration, was how it was done. The salesperson walked down the stairs and called in the order from the nearest phone booth. We were a salesperson's paradise in those days; we didn't even ask for better prices.

However, throughout the constant flow of merchandise from E. J. Korvette to customer, we were barraged with summonses from manufacturers who objected to the low discounting of their items. I simply stopped selling that brand in question and stocked competitive merchandise. Usually the competitor was happy to have fair-traded items working in E. J. Korvette. He was hungry for the business.

One day, about six months after we opened, while I was occupied with a big sale, an incident occurred that changed the course of E. J. Korvette. I was selling about $3000 worth of American Tourister luggage to a member of the Iraqi delegation to the U.N. They apparently used a great deal of luggage and spread the demand for it when they returned home. It was, in fact, beautiful luggage, and in those days we were selling it almost one-third cheaper than any of the New York department stores.

While I was waiting on my Iraqi customer, a tall, handsome, athletic-looking man walked in and stood about three feet away from me, listening to the conversation. He deserved that overworked adjective: suave. I looked away from my customer for a moment and asked, "May I help you?"

"I want to speak to you alone for a few minutes," he said.

"Do you want to sell me something?" I asked.

"I want to talk to you about small appliances—the whole gamut of small appliances, and some jewelry."

"You'll have to do what everyone else does," I told him. "You'll have to tell me what you've got, and I'll tell you what I need, and don't take up too much time."

"With all due respect," he said, "why don't you finish the sale and just give me a few minutes of your time? It will be well worth your while."

"No way. You tell me what you're selling and I'll either give you an order, or I won't. Then you come back every day, like everyone else."

He quietly looked at me, then calmly answered, "I'm going to sell you all the appliances you're currently buying, and I'm going to give you even better service. In addition, I'm going to give you an extra 10 percent discount."

When I heard this last sentence, I forgot about my customer and everything else. I grabbed him by the arm and took him downstairs, where we wouldn't be interrupted for the next 10 minutes. I was thinking, "Here I am, grossing about $1 million a year in this kind of merchandise, and here's a guy who says he's going to give me $100,000 during the course of a year. I could become a wealthy man."

It was no sales pitch. My visitor, Richard Polumbaum, kept his word and over the years we did a tremendous amount of business. He became one of the early heroes of my life. After we began to do business with him, we no longer had to think in terms of everything being an accommodation to luggage; our world now, not limited to luggage, was opening onto entirely new vistas.

We divided up the responsibilities and worked hard. I did most of the selling and buying. The remainder of the buying was done by Murray Beilenson, who was also in charge of the operational problem of getting the merchandise from the truck downstairs, up the steps and into the store. Since he was my first employee, it wasn't surprising that he had the worst job. Joe Zwillenberg, who did all the bookkeeping, was on the floor selling with the rest of us when he wasn't occupied with the books. All hands were constantly needed. George Yelen, our third employee, was also a strong influence on the floor and began to develop our business in major appliances, such as refrigerators and washing machines.

I hasten to add that we didn't try to lug these pieces of merchandise up the stairs. In the case of Thor washing machines, for example, we would place an order for a carload of 60, but they remained at the distributor's warehouse and as we sold each one, we would notify him. He made the delivery directly to the customer and assumed responsibility for servicing the machine during the first year. Delivery and servicing were included in our selling price. We sold about a carload of Thor washers every week because we were working on three dollars above cost, and we were buying them at the best possible price.

When E. J. Korvette first started, we completely disregarded percentages and thought only in terms of dollars. Everything we did was related to how many dollars or cents we would make on a specific item. Making money was really a simple thing to do because we ran a very tight ship. Our rent was about $550 a month. We knew exactly how many people we had working for us, and everyone was working all the time doing every conceivable kind of job in addition to his own. Consequently, we knew precisely in dollars and cents what it was costing us to run the store each week, each month, each year. Knowing our exact costs and keeping them to a minimum gave us the major advantage of being competitive to the point where no other retailer could think seriously of trying to match our prices.

Naturally, word of what we were doing got around town and created more than a little excitement in the retailing world. We began to attract attention wildly out of proportion to our small operation. Every department store in the city sent someone around to see what we were up to. The commercial newspapers gave us a great deal of space with stories explaining how we could do what we did. All this was the kind of publicity money couldn't buy.

Inevitably, with the amount of business we were doing, expansion was mandatory. Looking around in 1951, we found an empty store at Third Avenue and Forty-second Street which had been a Foltis-Fischer cafeteria. The store had 3,000 square feet of space, and the rent was $15,000 a year—low, considering that the amount of traffic within a radius of three or four blocks easily exceeded one million people daily. We signed a lease and started our second store there; the demand for our kind of business was so great that the new store had no adverse effect on the original store on Forty-sixth Street. By 1951, we had moved our Forty-sixth Street operation down to the first floor, which made everything much easier. We occupied two separate small stores at street level, with a total selling area of roughly 3,500 square feet. We were doing a total of $4.7 million annually, generating about a 10 percent pretax profit.

The second store was even more successful than the first. We added to the second store by taking an adjoining space around the corner on Forty-second Street. Between the first store and the expanded second store, we generated more than $5 million in volume from 1951 to 1952, with a profit before taxes of about $500,000. Our volume never dropped back. And, we still had not placed a word of advertising in a newspaper or in any other medium.

In those days, we were paying extremely generous salaries. Our general attitude was that we were a people's store operating with the benefit of an incredible amount of traffic. In order to maximize the store's productivity and limit the shrinkage and other factors that result from inept retailing, we decided from the beginning not only to pay more than the usual salaries, but to give out large bonuses at the end of the year paid across the board to everyone who was involved in the operation, which in 1952 numbered 30 employees.

By this time, too, we had organized ourselves. There was a central office for paying bills, but the two stores did their own individual buying. This was essential in view of the huge sales volume since local buying was the only way to insure having merchandise on the shelves all the time. Internally, the original spirit with which we began continued intact as we expanded. We were all very close, outside as well as inside the stores, with only rare exceptions. Working at E. J. Korvette was a way of life to our employees. It made a significant difference to us as a business. It was clear to everyone outside—the vendors, bankers and other professional retailers—that we enjoyed a remarkable *esprit de corps*.

By the end of 1952, we were on our way. We had two stores, both of them doing phenomenal business, and we began to see larger horizons opening ahead. We were ready to expand again.

2

The Rise to Success

As the two major E. J. Korvette stores boomed, I started to think about expansion and mergers as early as 1951. Looking to translate our performance into equity, I had serious conversations with other retailers. One of the first firms with which I talked was S. Klein's, a very successful discount department store specializing in soft lines (apparel). Richard Polumbaum, the man who helped raise my profits, initiated this negotiation with Spencer Allen, one of Klein's executives. I went to our first meeting with considerable anticipation, believing that Allen would say in effect, "Yes, we'd like to buy your company and bring you into the S. Klein operation, where we expect you to assume responsibility for the development of all our hard lines (appliances, etc.)."

That was what I expected. The reality of the meeting turned out to be quite different. Allen informed me that he was interested in our coming into Klein's as independent concessionaires. I was so disappointed and also inexperienced in negotiating that I'm afraid I became curt to the point of rudeness before our meeting ended. As a result, we never had any further relationship with S. Klein's.

Next, I initiated a meeting with Joe Weinstein, who had successfully built up May's Department Store in Brooklyn and was doing the same with another May's in Queens. May's was similar to Klein's. I wanted Weinstein to buy our business, use our personnel and our apparatus to develop the hard lines in his stores, which at that time were devoted exclusively to soft goods. Weinstein seemed uninterested, and this second attempt at a merger failed.

At this point, in early 1952, I decided to expand on my own, without outside help. A real estate broker called and asked if I would be interested in a great location in suburban White Plains. I knew nothing about White Plains, but I rode to the store with the agent. It was located on Mamaroneck Avenue, diagonally opposite Alexander's, an energetic and good volume-producing soft goods store, and in the immediate vicinity were branches of the finest New York Fifth Avenue shops. I realized at once the exceptional location and had no hesitation about taking it.

However, there was a problem. A closer inspection disclosed four feet of water in the store's basement. When we signed the lease the owners agreed to get rid of the water and to provide a sump pump in case the problem arose again. Fortunately, the water never returned.

Upon opening the White Plains store in December, 1952, we hadn't begun to think in terms of decor or anything that would give us an identity. In fact, both our stores had the cheapest fixtures—the White Plains store was aesthetically as drab and dark as the others. Our neighbors were understandably unhappy about the arrival of this ugly duckling discount store in their beautiful suburban shopping area. The air was thick with hostility; I remember feeling nervous when I walked down the street, conscious of how other merchants felt about me.

Of course, their objections were not entirely based on aesthetics. We were selling merchandise at a one-third discount across the board, and that hurt them. In fact, a shopkeeper in White Plains, in most cases, could buy merchandise cheaper from us than from a distributor because we bought in such large quantities.

I set up the White Plains store using the same basic plan I used in New York City. There were three men in charge of the store, with divided and overlapping responsibilities. I supervised the whole operation, and during the first year I spent all Saturday and Thursday at the store.

The White Plains store was modestly successful in the first year— its volume amounted to approximately $2 million. Like the New York City stores, the volume increased rapidly after that until it was soon generating about $5 million in volume, and showing a $500,000 pretax profit.

By the end of 1952, after four years of operation E. J. Korvette had three extremely profitable stores. Continued expansion was our goal; the momentum had begun. One night I decided to call all the employees together and discuss future directions. I spoke for an hour about this subject, and then announced I was ready to answer questions.

"What happens if we open another store and it loses money?" a man asked.

There was a long moment of complete silence. I was taken aback, and really didn't have an answer. Steadily increasing business, profits and volume seemed so inevitable, I took them for granted.

"It's impossible," I told my questioner. "We won't lose money. Forget it." It was inconceivable to me that we could ever lose money.

Often I've thought about why we were so successful. The reasons would apply to anyone anywhere in the United States who chooses to sell the classifications of merchandise I've talked about. He, too, could be substantially successful. It seems so obvious to me. We carried the best name-brand housewares, small appliances and watches. Moreover, we sold merchandise cheaper than anyone else because we had a lower cost of doing business—far below that of Macy's, Gimbel's or any other department store. They couldn't possibly meet our low prices, nor could they compete with our low overhead costs. E. J. Korvette's volume per square foot could not be matched.

The formula actually is a simple one and will be explained more fully in the second part of this book. If you choose to start your own small business, specifically in name-brand housewares, the first thing to do is to pick an extremely inexpensive location, whether it be a store in a small town, in a city or even in your home or garage. If you sell desirable, identifiable brands of housewares cheaper than anyone else, you will make money. But you must remember to think in terms of dollars rather than percentages.

For example, today there's a well-known set of Farberware pots that department stores sell for about $85. It costs $53. If you sell this set for $55 and in the course of a week sell 100 sets, you can gross $200.

This was the theory I started out with and it has never changed. At the end of a week, it's necessary to avoid saying, "I only worked at a 2 percent markup," but rather say, "I grossed $200." This is the way an individual starting from scratch with limited funds ought to begin a business. The initial stock could be housewares, hardware, automotive equipment, jewelry, books, records or any combination of these items.

The chief obstacle preventing anyone from building the kind of retailing empire that I did, is a failure to apply purpose, energy and intelligence. Many people would have stopped if they had been in my position after the first four years. Why did I push on? First, because I have obsessive ambition; and second, I have always had an inordinate curiosity. I am naturally an adventurer. And finally, I must admit, there is the matter of ego, which successful entrepreneurs always have in large quantities. In my case, I must add a kind of naiveté; it never occurred to me that I couldn't do anything I decided I wanted to do.

Another ingredient must also be accounted for. When everything you do is met with incredible success, a powerful momentum is created. A supreme confidence is generated that constantly says, "If I can do no wrong, why not go forward?" It's certainly true that success breeds success. It is infectious. Some people call it luck, but to me it seems there is more than chance involved. A young man who developed our jewelry business once said to me, "Gene, if you fell into a barrel of manure, you'd come up with a gold bar." Maybe so, but once you've fallen into the barrel and found the bar, the other barrels hold out the hope of being equally productive.

For me, I believe that any success was the result of a happy marriage of my personality with the integrity, intelligence and creativity of the people with whom I surrounded myself from the beginning. A handful of these people are still very much involved in the retail world, and they are considered to be among the best. I was unbelievably lucky to find these people. Later on, I wasn't as lucky and hired some who were inept, inadequate, selfish or dishonest. Sometimes it seemed I got more than my share. By then, however, the business had been laid and developed on the soundest human foundations.

It has sometimes been said in the retail world, I "cleaned out the poolrooms" for my help. This isn't the literal truth, but it is true that as we grew and expanded so rapidly, every week we were in need of new people. Friends brought in friends, family brought in family. No doubt, among all these people there were some hangers-on, but most of them went back to the green table before long. They simply could not survive in our business.

On the other hand, it was entirely possible for people in our organization to find their own level of responsibility and authority. I was constantly talking with my employees and was aware of their individual thrusts. I observed what was happening with them from day to day, and was easily able to tell whether or not they were successful in their jobs. But, that was at the beginning. As the business grew larger, the close contact could no longer be maintained.

I was aware that it was highly dangerous to bring in someone who said to me, in effect, "I'm a veritable genius, and if you give me a big budget and let me develop a do-it-yourself shop in all your stores, I can make a lot of money for you." If I heard that, I learned—*caveat emptor*. How could I tell whether a man who portrayed himself as an all-knowing merchandiser was what he claimed to be, or if he was absolutely unworthy of such responsibility? For all I knew, he could do irreparable harm to the company.

This was not yet a problem after those first four years, as I looked to expand to a new location. In late 1952, something turned up almost at once. A large European department store group, known as C. and A. Brenninkmeyer, opened a store on Fifth Avenue and Thirty-eighth Street. It consisted of a selling basement, main floor and escalators to the second floor, but it was an outright failure. Hearing about its plight, we met with the Europeans and they agreed to relinquish the premises to us. Along with giving them several months security, we were to pay an exorbitant rental of $185,000 a year.

We almost made a mistake, but were saved by a technicality. The leases were drawn up, and we met in the Brenninkmeyer offices to sign them. Reading through for the last time, I found myself concerned with one clause—the one that described the possible uses of the premises. Actually, it didn't really matter what it said, because there was no doubt that the premises would have a general usage. But for some inexplicable reason, the Brenninkmeyers and their lawyers decided to restrict the usage clause to ladies' lingerie and hosiery. We could have occupied the premises and simply sold what we wanted, but that clause made me hesitate. I knew we weren't ready for this kind of move, if it turned out that we were, in fact, restricted. Looking back, I don't think it would have been a disaster, because we could have written a huge volume in that space. But at that point we didn't have the merchandising acumen in soft lines to properly utilize that much area. It seemed we had no right to consider such a high rental and enormous space without soft goods knowledge. I believed this, even though we had already been flirting with soft goods lines in men's pants, shirts, ties, socks, handkerchiefs and some women's lingerie.

Thinking about the problem, I turned to one of the Brenninkmeyers and said, "This is a lot of money you're asking for rent and security. This usage clause," I went on, "doesn't categorically say that we are permitted to sell general merchandise, but it seems to imply restrictions of some kind. We're going to have to change the usage clause."

To my astonishment, Brenninkmeyer turned to me and curtly said, "Take care of it yourself."

I was annoyed and slightly affronted by his tone and manner. We broke off the meeting with the leases unsigned, and I returned to my office. (I use the word "office" loosely; it was a little room used principally by the controller to pay the bills.) When I got there, a phone call was waiting for me from a broker. He told me he had a store with about 4,000 square feet of space available on Forty-eighth Street between Fifth and Sixth avenues facing the skating rink at Rockefeller Center. As soon as I arrived in the landlord's office, I began negotiating the rental; we signed the lease within 48 hours.

It was a superb location.

In setting up this fourth store, I proceeded differently than I had with the others. I treated it as a cooperative, asking for contributions and capitalizing the store for $350,000. It was not difficult. Every store we had opened was a separate corporation, and this one was to be E. J. Korvette 48th Street, Inc. I let it be known that I wanted to raise $350,000, and invited everyone to participate. "Everyone" included friends, relatives, employees, vendors and others who were interested. I put up $25,000 of the total, representing the voting stock, and the remainder was non-voting common stock. I was never involved with the details. My controller and his assistant handled everything.

I might add E. J. Korvette didn't actually need outside money. This financing plan for the fourth store represented a kind of conservatism on my part, although I don't consider myself a conservative person. But, I simply didn't want to encroach upon the resources of the other stores. They were all doing well on their own and I wanted the fourth store to also operate on its own.

However, for the first time in organizing a store, I found I had made a big mistake. I overestimated this location, which I thought was the best one of all. It was only three blocks from the Forty-sixth Street store, but its proximity to the Radio City complex with all the traffic around it led me to believe we would write $8 million a year in business there—especially with 4,000 square feet of working space. To my surprise, we never reached that figure, although we did come close—$6 million the first year.

In 1953, shortly after we began business on Forty-eighth Street, we opened a fifth store in a drab, shoddy former Grand Union supermarket, facing a cemetery in Hempstead, Long Island. It offended my own and other people's aesthetic senses, but at that particular time, the bargains on merchandise sold didn't permit such considerations. If there was a choice between aesthetics or pragmatism, there could be no contest.

As we did in White Plains, we opened this fifth store in an excellent suburban shopping area not far from one of the great suburban department stores in the United States—Abraham & Strauss in Hempstead. A&S was not happy to see us open because there was no question that at least to some extent we would soon be shaking them up. Realistically, we weren't hurting their volume or their profitability to a great degree, but in our mutually competitive departments we were cutting into their business.

We were dealing, as always, in the same classifications of identifiable merchandise. But A&S was maintaining the manufacturer's fair-traded or suggested list prices. To the extent that we discounted that merchandise, we took away from their business.

Like most of the big department stores in America, a great store like A&S doesn't depend on this minimal amount of identifiable merchandise for its success. What makes a department store great is the quantity of fashion apparel and home decorating merchandise it sells. There are many first-class department stores in this country that don't carry, sell, and are not even interested in identifiable goods such as housewares, small appliances, jewelry, radios, automotive accessories, hardware and similar items. That was why we didn't really shake the financial structure of the A&S giant in Hempstead, even though we were soon doing a huge volume of business in the same town.

What bothered A&S was that they couldn't fully accommodate their own customers. People would come to their store to buy a sweater, jacket, coat, dress, sportswear or some related item, but they would come to us to buy a watch, iron, toaster or pots and pans. We carved out our own niche, and it caused A&S some discomfort. The shakeup was not financial but centered in the outlook of A&S's management. For the first time they became aware of this neglected part of their customer franchise, and in later years they began to improve, making a tremendous effort to be competitive with E. J. Korvette in every possible way. They watched every move we made and profited from it. In my opinion, they remain the finest department store in the Greater New York area.

A&S watched with amazement after we opened the store in Hempstead. This ugly little store wrote $5 million worth of business in its first year of operation, and generated $500,000 pretax profit. The whole chain was doing a volume of $20 million annually, throwing off a pretax profit of approximately $2 million. More than $1 million was distributed among all employees in the form of bonuses. There were no exceptions. The minimum bonus was $1,000; at the top, bonuses ran as high as $60,000 per individual.

The White Plains store came about essentially by accident because a broker had space to sell. In Hempstead, we proceeded with the assumption that we could do no wrong. After our success there, we began to talk seriously about starting a department store of our own. On my way to the Hempstead location I passed a potato field, and it wasn't long before I was thinking about the possibilities of that field as a location for a store. I can't honestly say that I foresaw the world of shopping centers, but that potato field in the area known as Carle Place near Westbury, Long Island, seemed a fine location for a department store. Today, one can look at the great shopping center there to see how valid that idea turned out to be.

In August, 1954, we were financially prepared for the move to Westbury. We found ourselves involved with new young developers, Kane and Schwartz, who were engaged in building homes on Long Island. We reached an understanding and signed a lease. They would build a department store with three floors, 30,000 square feet to a floor, on the potato field.

I had disregarded aesthetics before, at considerable cost to my vanity, but this time I meant to do things differently. The Hempstead store continued to offend me; though the store was profitable, I couldn't wait to close it.

At this juncture, a young man named Bernard Waltzer attracted my attention. He was our outside accountant and was becoming eloquent on the subject of going public. We had several conversations about this, and I began to entertain the idea seriously.

Meanwhile, we made the necessary financial arrangements with the builders and they produced our new Westbury department store in an incredibly short time. Although this store was in Carle Place, I always refer to it as my Westbury store. It had escalators, splendid illumination, excellent fixtures and an outside parking lot for 500 cars. It is hard to believe in terms of today, but work on this store began immediately after we signed the lease in August, 1954, and it opened on December 2, 1954—a remarkable feat. Everyone deserved a great deal of credit for this accomplishment, but I gave special thanks to the store fixture people, in those days known as Hochberg Brothers (now HBSA Industries). They made it possible, working around the clock, to finish on time. Later, they did all our store fixturing, and today are probably the largest such company in the United States.

Our basic format for setting up this new venture didn't change. It was, as always, a separate corporation, a department store separate and distinct from the rest of the company. There were no outside guarantors. The total capitalization for this venture was $500,000. Again, the call went out to everyone who might be interested in joining us. A prospective investor had only to look at what we were doing to see that he could hardly find a better place to put his money.

In spite of the fact that the Forty-eighth Street store hadn't reached my expectations when it opened, it became in 1954 my most successful venture. Just before we opened in Westbury, we paid a 30 percent dividend to all the stockholders in the Forty-eighth Street store, and several hundred thousand dollars in bonuses to the employees. We took another $100,000 from the initial funding and invested it in the Westbury store on behalf of the original Forty-eighth Street stockholders.

I put $100,000 into the Westbury operation myself, and we gave the landlord $100,000 as advance rent, which he promptly reinvested as a stockholder in our stores. As a result of all this activity, with added money coming in from vendors and others, we easily put together the $500,000 capitalization we needed. We returned the total investment in the first year of operation.

By 1955, I had come a long way from my first store on Forty-sixth Street. I financed that store myself and there was no additional financing for the next one on Forty-second Street: its bills were paid at Forty-sixth Street. I owned all the stock in both places. Then, White Plains became part of the central structure, and after that, Long Island. The profits were very high, but they were well divided in bonuses. I was making well over $100,000 a year. The older and more successful I became, the smaller the salary I took.

In breaking away from the image I established as owner of four "shabby" stores, I could look then in 1955 at the carpeted main floor in Westbury, listen to the hum of escalators, glance around the 90,000 square feet of merchandise and watch the cars drive into the parking lot. This was satisfying enough, but what happened as soon as the store opened was a tremendous boost to my pragmatic side.

We were totally unprepared for the overwhelming success of the new store. On the day it opened, the customers poured in so rapidly that the situation was out of control at times. With 116 employees on the selling staff, we did $138,000 the first day. Between December 2 and Christmas day we took in more than $2 million. It was a spectacular effort; we turned over the stock three or four times. The Christmas season no doubt was a factor, but it was far from being the only reason for our success.

For one thing, the E. J. Korvette organization had put the right people in charge, choosing from the best of our managerial personnel. We set up a modest buying structure, operating out of Westbury, and were able to keep up with the unprecedented demand for merchandise. Our popularity with customers and vendors alike grew every day.

Selling soft goods was the major departure made at this point. For the first time, an E. J. Korvette store had soft goods departments— ladies' dresses, ladies' sportswear, men's apparel, men's furnishings, shoe departments, children's departments and layettes. To professionals in the field, our efforts probably seemed amateurish. Nevertheless, we had a full-line department store—a working combination of hard and soft goods.

In one respect, things were the same. Identifiable merchandise like housewares and all the hard lines were doing an extraordinary volume of business. The traffic generated in these departments rubbed off on all the others.

We discovered, however, that we had a unique problem in our soft wares division. We wanted name-brand apparel, but none of the soft ware manufacturers would sell to us because they didn't want their lines discounted. We solved this problem by having three of our most experienced people buy, as best they could, from other retailers in New York and out of town. There were two immediate results: First, big sales because of the recognizable labels on the clothes we bought; we were the first to discount these labels on the scale I'm describing. The second result was action taken by the manufacturers who wanted to protect their reputations with the other department stores in the New York metropolitan area. They were compelled to send people to the Westbury store to buy everything off the racks that bore their labels.

This left us with an old problem, but this time with soft goods— trying to maintain adequate stock. We had no choice except to offer our own unbranded apparel line as the best product for the money, rather than as a fine label discount. The name-brand merchandise was not available to us, and we were so large now, there was no way of buying sufficient quantities to operate day by day.

Our major thrust in apparel really began at Westbury; our first five stores were too small for this, ranging in size from 3,000 to 10,000 square feet. The success of the department store soon produced other unexpected business. Two bright young men came to us and said they would like to open a large furniture and carpet showroom (approximately 50,000 square feet) across the street from our store. If they succeeded in creating this structure, they wanted us to permit them to use the E. J. Korvette name for which we would get a percentage of their sales.

We agreed, and the results were other lucrative sources of income. In their first year, they reached a volume of $7 million, and paid us more than $200,000. At the same time, we arranged to build a luncheonette adjoining the main operation—it was actually a part of our parking lot—and that little enterprise of 800 square feet netted us $35,000 a year.

The most unusual development was giving permission to a pretzel merchant who paid us $15,000 annually to sell his product in the rear of our parking lot. He must have done well; he once wanted to give the manager of our Westbury store a beautiful new Chrysler, but the gift was refused.

With five small stores in operation, and the success of our first department store, I began to listen more closely to Bernard Waltzer's arguments for going public. I decided definitely to do it and proposed a plan to close all five of our original small stores and replace them with department stores. Another part of the plan was to begin building a huge national retail business.

Meanwhile, we were not entirely free of operating difficulties. One of the worst problems was the harassment in White Plains. There, the town police were ever vigilant in front of our building to prevent deliveries of merchandise. No truck was permitted to pull up, stop and unload because of traffic regulations. To get the merchandise into the store, we had to rent space on a yearly basis in a parking lot a block away. We employed three persons who unloaded deliveries at the rented parking lot and carried merchandise to the store all day. I don't know who was responsible for this situation, but in White Plains that was the way the ball game had to be played. This harassment was inconvenient and uncomfortable, but we recognized that with the kind of business we were doing in White Plains, we could afford to overlook this situation.

What annoyed me even more was the fact that cars were not permitted to stop in front of our store. If a husband and wife drove up and the husband stopped to let his wife out to go shopping, he was in danger of getting a ticket. To save our customers that embarrassment, we put a man on the sidewalk to wave cars away.

These unpleasantries made that store a difficult operation. In order to cope with the problems of merchandise logistics, the manager spent a good deal of his time outside the store every day, regardless of the weather. This left him unfamiliar with what was happening inside. In spite of these difficulties, to my amazement, the store kept on making excellent profits.

Unfortunately, we also had a similar situation in the town of Hempstead. There, too, the local police would not permit trucks to stop in front of our store. It was necessary to do the unloading at the rear in spite of the fact that we had no facilities for receiving there. Again, we had to hire extra personnel to compensate.

None of these problems stood in the way of going public. We made these plans with the help of Bernard Waltzer, the driving force behind the move, and Ed Friedman, our house lawyer, who became someone very special in our lives. He was a marvelous man and bore the brunt of the formidable legal difficulties which plagued us throughout these early years. He did his job efficiently and in a way that never disturbed our ability to concern ourselves exclusively with the art of making money.

One of the worst problems Ed Friedman helped us through was our difficulty with the fair-trade laws. In the forties and fifties, these laws were strictly enforced in New York State. Most brand names in the small appliance and jewelry fields were fair-traded, which meant the manufacturer established a selling price at retail level for a specific piece of merchandise and the retailer was obligated to sell the item at the prescribed price.

When we began our business, we were not very familiar with the fair-trade laws. Consequently, we sold all our fair-traded merchandise at our regular discount of 33⅓ percent off the manufacturer's list price. As a result, we had many threats of lawsuits, and several attempts at injunctions were made by the manufacturers. If we had known all the legal ramifications of the laws, we would have thought twice before selling this merchandise at reduced prices. Complaints from manufacturers were numerous, and at one point a wholesale distributor advised us that we would be better off closing the store and moving to Florida.

Ed Friedman told us not to worry about our legal difficulties and to keep on selling the merchandise while he fought for us in court. His strategy was to delay any court action, which would permit us to go on selling below fair-traded prices. Nevertheless, there were times when process servers knocked at the doors of all the E. J. Korvette corporate officers. Once an officer was served with an injunction, we were not allowed to cut the price of the merchandise listed in it. Consequently, we all worked hard to avoid being served. One of our executives even slipped out through a trap door onto the roof of his garden apartment, and then left the building through the door of his neighbor's apartment, to avoid a process server stationed at his door.

Occasionally, when we were enjoined by a manufacturer from selling a product that was vital to our business, we went as far as possible to get the injunction lifted. One of the defenses open was to prove that the manufacturer was not policing the price fixing of his product in other stores. We sent out people to other retailers, in an attempt to purchase the product at reduced prices.

One particularly tough manufacturer was determined to keep the retailers in line, and we found it extremely hard to buy his merchandise below fair-traded prices. His line was important to us, and we didn't want to lose it. We sent one of our salesmen to the Brooks Uniform Company, where he rented a South American army officer's uniform. Dressed in this bogus military attire, our salesperson visited several retailers and purchased the manufacturer's merchandise at discount prices, even persuading the retailers to give him an invoice showing the discounts. As a result, when our case with this manufacturer came to court, we were able to get the injunction lifted.

To return to our process of going public—we began by first consulting with Lehman Brothers in 1954, since this house was well known for its cooperation with the retail community in America and was considered to be the banking house for retailers.

They appeared glad to see us, told us they had been impressed by our performance to date and expressed a willingness to become our banking house and take us to the public. They recommended to us a new auditing firm, Eisner & Lubin, which we hired immediately, and a law firm, Simpson, Thacher and Bartlett, to represent us as a public corporation. From this law firm a young man named Richard M. Dicke was assigned to work with us. From that point on, he had a great influence on my career at E. J. Korvette. I only regret that I did not always take his advice. If I had, I might have completely carried out my plan to make E. J. Korvette a national organization. Dicke came to us at a time when we needed a very capable attorney because of the increasing complexity of our operations. It was always a great comfort for me to have him at my side, ready to take on any problem.

It was only a few weeks after we had gone to Simpson, Thacher and Bartlett that we had a call from Lehman Brothers. At the meeting we held at their request they informed us with regret that they were under considerable pressure from the established retail community and would have to forego being our banking house. I asked them to recommend someone else, but I can't recall whether it was they or someone in my organization who suggested Carl M. Loeb, Rhoades & Co. In any case, fortunately for us, we took our business to them.

At Loeb, Rhoades there was no problem. They were not identified with the retailing community and were involved in engineering and many other things not directly related to the retail business. They were interested and rather intrigued by what we proposed to do and hired a great retailer named Richard "Bob" Weil Jr. to make an evaluation of E. J. Korvette. I was invited to take him on a tour of the chain so that he could return with an opinion. Meanwhile, two young men, Stanley Grant and Tom Kempner, were assigned to us from Loeb, Rhoades.

After traveling with Bob Weil through the stores, I had the feeling he had looked askance at what we represented. He had been considered a young genius at 28 when he was president of Bamberger's in New Jersey. Soon after that, he was brought in as president of Macy's. He had also written a book, *The Age of Philosophy*.

At Macy's he decided that he would not permit the store to become a showroom for the growing number of discount stores proliferating in the city and took direct action—he began to do his own discounting. This brought on a price war with Gimbel's and led Macy's owner, the Straus family, to conclude that the Macy image had been damaged. Weil was asked to resign, and he became a consultant to Loeb, Rhoades.

I could not shake the feeling he was singularly unimpressed with what he had seen, certainly in terms of E. J. Korvette's physical properties. I felt that he would not recommend us to Loeb, Rhoades. The next day, one of the firm's executives called and said, "It's Bob Weil's opinion that you are the future Sears, Roebuck of the United States." From that moment, there was no doubt Loeb, Rhoades was going to be our adviser in all our financial affairs.

To this day, I don't understand how Weil arrived at his decision. After we went public, I hired him as a consultant to E. J. Korvette, and if he had not died soon after, we would have had a long relationship. He gave us experience and wisdom impossible to replace.

After all the anticipation, going public, as it turned out, was a routine undertaking. In 1955, when we went public, our stock was sold at $10 a share and the stock sold out quickly; shortly afterward, in 1956, it went to approximately $28 a share. We raised $2 million from the public for the corporation, of which E. J. Korvette and its employees controlled over half. Loeb, Rhoades acquired 75,000 warrants, exercisable at approximately $10 a share.

After we went public, we had a large amount of money available to us. All the stores that had been individual corporations were brought together into a single unit. I began to spend at least half my time trying to develop new locations for the future. We were no longer thinking about small stores, but more in terms of 100,000-square-foot stores— even larger, if necessary. We were not yet oriented toward warehousing or redistribution centers. Consequently, the design for our new stores assumed that we would use 60,000 of the 100,000 square feet for selling, and 40,000 for the stock and marking areas and other backup uses necessary to a retail facility.

In the late 1950s we opened stores in West Islip, Long Island, containing 80,000 square feet; in Scarsdale, New York, with about 100,000 square feet; and in New Brunswick, New Jersey, on U.S. 1, with a little over 80,000 square feet. We also rented a huge former department store in Hartford, Connecticut, with about 200,000 square feet. Then we opened a downtown store in Brooklyn on Fulton Street, previously an Oppenheim-Collins outlet owned by City Stores. It had been doing badly, and we rented the space for an extremely low figure; for us it became a tremendous moneymaker. Finally, we opened a store of 100,000 square feet in Springfield, Pennsylvania—our first venture in that state.

The opening of all these stores made it difficult for us to maintain our previous profits. At the time we went public, we were generating approximately $1,380,000 net, but in the first few years after the expansion, we found it hard to improve on this figure because we were more than doubling our expenses. Moreover, startup costs for the new stores, not only on the spot but in the home office, specifically in merchandising, were pyramiding at a rate that had a depressing effect on our earnings. They dipped down as far as $900,000.

This decline frightened much of the financial community, and our stock dropped to $9 a share. It was in this period that Loeb, Rhoades' warrants were to expire, and since the exercise price was higher than the existing market price, it was a disappointment to our investment bankers.

In large part, our position could be attributed to simple inexperience. My own background was that of an entrepreneur in a small luggage shop. All the people around me, with only a few exceptions, were nonprofessionals who had been in the Army and had come out looking for jobs. In spite of the fact that so many of them were highly competent workers, they still lacked a certain sophistication that was necessary for the arena E. J. Korvette was now occupying.

I was very concerned about my continuing relationship with Loeb, Rhoades. By this time, they were an everyday need in everything I did. I leaned on them constantly, either in their offices or on the phone. We were always in communication. Before Bob Weil died, I discussed the problem with him, and we decided to go to Lehman Brothers to talk about what might be done.

Lehman Brothers indicated that it was important for our budding young retail vehicle to retain its important relationship with Loeb, Rhoades. It was suggested further that we extend the warrants for two years, with Loeb, Rhoades paying a premium of approximately $.75 per warrant for this extension. We adopted this plan happily and Loeb, Rhoades was certainly pleased. The stockholders approved it unanimously.

While I and many people around me were disappointed that our profits had dipped to the $900,000 level, our performance had been quite good. I was naive enough to overlook completely the expenses we had incurred in more than doubling the existing volume, and I failed to understand them. Viewed in perspective, the fact is that we had achieved tremendous growth at a relatively small cost.

In 1956, plunging ahead, we opened three new stores—at Camp
Hill, near Harrisburg, Pennsylvania; on Route 22 in New Jersey; and
in Northeast Philadelphia, near the Penn Fruit Distribution Center.
With the opening of these stores, plus improving figures in the existing
stores, everything began to come together. Profits quickly jumped back
to $1.5 million, then to $1.8 million and eventually into a $3.9 million
net profit by the end of 1956.

At the point when Loeb, Rhoades had to exercise their warrants or
let them expire, E. J. Korvette stock had climbed to $160 per share. I
never knew when and how many of the warrants were exercised. I do
know that it was a profitable experience for our investment bankers
and everyone was pleased.

Further developments for our future were taking shape. Thousands
of "inhouse" stockholders—employees, their families, the vendors and
so on—had made a huge amount of money on their investment in E. J.
Korvette stock, and that was highly satisfying. The image of the business had changed quite radically. The orginal, small, shabby specialty
stores had been replaced by aesthetically attractive and exciting small
department stores. The merchandising was much more sophisticated.
We had gone into the retail community and hired many reputable
people. The business was taking shape handsomely and successfully.
The mid-fifties was a happy time; we were big winners. Everyone was
pleased, even the stockholders. The annual meetings were pleasant
affairs where few complaints were heard.

Naturally, all this was well known in the retailing world, and
other corporations had begun to look at us covetously. It was time for
the mating dance to begin again.

3

Mergers—and More Mergers

OUR FIRST FEELER IN THE MERGER MARKET came from Joe Weinstein of May's, who was still developing a well-run soft goods department store in Brooklyn, New York. In 1951, he had asked for a meeting, but at the time I was not interested in merging with May's as we did not complement each other geographically. Both chains had expanded into Long Island and there was only a two-block distance between the stores in Brooklyn on Fulton Street.

In my opinion, Joe Weinstein was the best of what I call the unique merchants of New York. New York City was unusual compared to the rest of the country. It produced large department stores which reflected the personalities and talents of individual people as contrasted with the usual faceless department store chains. For example, New York had given retailing Nathan Ohrbach and Ohrbach's, George Farkas and Alexander's, and J.W. May's, with Weinstein as the principal entrepreneur.

After our initial meeting in 1951, Weinstein and I had several more meetings with merger in mind; I had become more anxious to translate our performance into equity. At least one of the meetings was very disturbing, not because of anything that was said, but because he sneezed into my lasagna, and I was hungry. On that particular day, he didn't have a chance at a merger with me.

Joe Weinstein was a seven-day-a-week dedicated retailer. He was an unusual man and there is a large inventory of stories about him. In his own way, he was a kind of local tyrant; he ran his store like a private kingdom. It is rumored that before the store opened in the morning, the employees had to stand at attention and sing, "For He's a Jolly Good Fellow," after which they sang "God Bless America." While this was going on, Weinstein would walk around the store to see if he found anyone who was not standing at attention and singing with enthusiasm.

I went to see him one day in his Brooklyn store, taking with me a merchandising woman who didn't know him. She was an extremely capable person who, unfortunately, didn't stay with me very long. As we went into the store, we could hear him bellowing at some hapless employee at the top of his lungs, his voice sounding loud and clear in this busy downtown department store: "You're a buyer; you're a shit!"

On another day, he was walking through his store and found one of his buyers on crutches. "What's the matter?" he inquired. The man explained to J. W. (as he preferred to be called) that he had been playing handball and injured his ankle, but not wanting to miss any time at work, he had come on crutches. "You're fired!" Weinstein yelled at him. "Take your crutches and get out of here."

I tell these stories to give you an idea of what kind of man Joe Weinstein was, but he was undeniably successful. His downtown store in Brooklyn and his several suburban stores were all clean, first-rate places, with excellent merchandise and always a lot of it. He ran a tight ship and diligently scrutinized every detail of the operation. The performance of May's stock was highly successful, and during the years I knew Weinstein, anyone who was fortunate enough to own it made a lot of money.

His chief rival was George Farkas, the owner of Alexander's. This store had an enviable reputation. It had begun in the Bronx, moved to the suburban area of White Plains, and then, to Weinstein's consternation, into Rego Park, Queens. Until that time there appeared to be an understanding between Farkas and Weinstein that Brooklyn and Queens were to be May's territory, while the Bronx and Westchester would be Alexander's territory.

Consequently, when Farkas opened his store in Rego Park, it led to an undeclared war. The bitterness that arose between the two men was so great that when I met with both of them later in 1955 to discuss the possible merger of May's, Alexander's and E. J. Korvette (a merger of great interest to me), I had to sit between them. Farkas was visibly afraid of being attacked by Weinstein.

That was a serious merger meeting, at least as far as Weinstein and I were concerned. Farkas had a unique arrangement in the case of his controlling interest of Alexander's, and if a merger were to occur, it would not leave him in a desirable position. He had taken his equity and created a trust for his four sons, equally. As long as he and his wife, Ruth, were alive, they would be in control; but if the business went public or was merged, the trust would be ended and the sons would be in possession of the equity, leaving the father in quite a different position at Alexander's. I didn't know about all of this until the end of the merger talks when Farkas related all of the above to me.

The 1955 meeting with Farkas and Weinstein was inconclusive, but conversations went on intermittently. Meanwhile, I had other meetings with Joe Weinstein, in which he sought to merge with E. J. Korvette, but without Alexander's. At one point, a grand plan evolved to merge Ohrbach's, Alexander's, May's and E. J. Korvette. Geographically, that would have been a good idea. There was a small conflict between E. J. Korvette and Alexander's, but it was not significant, and the other chains were operating in separate areas.

It was an ingenious plan. We would have E. J. Korvette integrate the hard lines in all the other locations, making them full-line department stores. The result could have been a 30 to 40 percent addition to existing volume, a substantial gain. In addition, we would permit the others to assume full responsibility for our existing soft goods operation as well as its future development. If accomplished, such a merger would have been the nucleus for a great department store chain in cities all over the country. It would have been a well-organized, in-motion, soft and hard goods merchandising team.

Without undue modesty, I can say truthfully that I was the only one who could have made this merger possible because the other three men involved represented a mass of conflicting egos. Nathan Ohrbach was a fine merchant; George Farkas was extremely good with numbers, but I thought him the weakest link in the chain; and Joe Weinstein was a superb retailer who thrived on his business. In fact, Joe's whole life was completely centered in his stores. What might have been the torture of complex detail for someone else, was sublime pleasure for him.

Still, among the four of us, I was the only one who could have put it together. I wanted to do it, and I tried—very hard. More than once, I used Loeb, Rhoades to get the people together and attempt to make it work. My relationship with Joe Weinstein was on-and-off as far as merger was concerned. I also tried to make an individual deal with George Farkas, and I spent a considerable amount of time with Nathan Ohrbach. But I could never find a way to put the package together. I still think it was a great loss. It would have been a marvelous merger and, under the laws prevailing at the time, I believe the government would have permitted it.

The obstacle that couldn't be overcome, as I've indicated, was the way George Farkas had structured his equity in Alexander's. He was not prepared to make the sacrifice of losing his personal control at the store. I argued the point over and over with him and his family, with no effect.

I didn't really want to merge with May's if Alexander's was not a part of the deal. If it had been, there is no question that I could have come to an agreement easily with Joe Weinstein. I was so hellbent on Alexander's because I thought they had the best reputation even though they had the smallest earnings. May's always had the best earnings, second to Korvette, and Ohrbach's closely followed, with Alexander's far at the bottom. Nevertheless, I was fascinated by Alexander's; I loved their stores, their presentation, their reputation.

It was an infatuation that blinded me to the facts. I believe now, that if I had never met Farkas, never concentrated on Alexander's, but focused on Ohrbach's and showed a little more wisdom and sophistication, I could have made a package of Ohrbach's, May's and E. J. Korvette which would have been just as good, whether or not Alexander's had been included. But all that, of course, is hindsight.

Still disconcerted at the loss of a triple merger, I bought 43 percent of Alexander's stock in 1955 for $9.7 million. It was sold in 1968 by E. J. Korvette for $23.5 million.

In my quest for merger with Ohrbach's in 1958, Lehman Brothers set up the first meeting between myself and Nathan Ohrbach, a man some 25 years my senior. The meeting at our Philadelphia store did not go well, which was my fault because I handled him with a lack of respect. Later that year I had a second meeting, this time with Nathan's son, Jerry Ohrbach.

At this meeting, again organized by Lehman Brothers, Jerry Ohrbach disclosed to me that their earnings that year were $800,000 net. Up to that point, I don't believe they had ever earned $1 million. I indicated to him that I thought we ought to merge, and that E. J. Korvette was prepared to give them $15 million in stock. I believed that was a reasonable offer, and while I had no feeling it would be accepted, it seemed to me at least a beginning.

A few weeks later, I heard that C.&A. Brenninkmeyer, still trying to get on the American scene properly, efficiently and quickly, had bought Ohrbach's for $25 million cash. Obviously, I had come in too late with too little.

Some years later, in 1970, after I had retired from E. J. Korvette, I met Nathan Ohrbach again, but this time under tragic circumstances.

He had suffered a severe stroke which had made him speechless and motionless. He could hear, but the only mobility left to him was in his eyes. By a sad coincidence, my mother suffered a stroke at the same time. That year, I found myself spending every Sunday from early in the morning until about two o'clock in the afternoon with Nathan Ohrbach and my mother, in the little park that was part of University Hospital. I talked to Nathan about the old days, and one afternoon remarked to him, "Isn't it a pity, Nathan, that we never merged? I'll bet we would have been great together." Tears welled up in his eyes, the only answer he could make, but plainly he agreed.

I spent the better part of his last year with him. Not long before he died, his nurse, who was devoted to him, turned to me one day and observed that Nathan thought of me as a son. I was proud of that.

While the grand May's-Korvette-Ohrbach's-Alexander's plan never came to fruition, other doors opened in different directions. Not long after we went public in 1956, I was asked to meet with a colorful and well-known personality, Albert M. Greenfield, the head of Bankers' Securities, which controlled the chain called City Stores. This chain consisted of department stores and specialty shops strung up and down the Atlantic coast and as far west as New Orleans. Probably the best known of these properties was the Maison Blanche department store group in New Orleans, but there were other popular divisions—Litt Brothers in Philadelphia; the McCrory variety stores; the Franklin Simon and Oppenheim Collins specialty shops in the New York metropolitan area, among others.

Greenfield, when I met him, looked to me like a sitting Buddha. He saw everything in terms of real estate, and he was essentially a giant in that field. He had become so heavily involved with real estate in the Philadelphia area that he was known there as "Mr. Philadelphia." Someone from his staff came to me and suggested a meeting, at which Greenfield offered to buy E. J. Korvette for about half of the going market price. I didn't know whether he was serious or pulling my leg in making such a ludicrous offer, and decided I wouldn't take him too seriously.

Whenever I find myself in someone else's organization, I'm always aware of the atmosphere that permeates it, the aura it emanates. In Greenfield's case it seemed to me the people around him were extremely frightened of him. I could understand why they might be afraid of this paunchy, short, overbearing, tyrannical man, who reminded me of Sydney Greenstreet. Once, when I was going down to meet with him, an executive of an investment company jokingly told me, "Eugene, if you're going to see that old pirate, keep your goddamn hands in your pockets." I learned that this was not an uncommon feeling about him.

What I remember most about our first meeting, was that Greenfield spit eight feet through the air and missed the spittoon in the middle of the floor. I would say his spitting ability matched his retail acumen—he never hit the mark. His son, Gordon, who was president of the Franklin Simon-Oppenheim Collins specialty shops, proved to be a different kind of person. I met him in Florida one day by chance, and we came back to New York on the same plane. We talked and he told me he hoped his father and I would get together and complete our deal to merge City Stores and E. J. Korvette. I thought he was a likeable, intelligent, easygoing young man; no one would ever have thought he was Albert Greenfield's son.

"Gordon," I said, "there's no sense meeting with your old man, because he's only going to make me a ridiculous offer, and we'd just be wasting each other's time."

"Please, Gene," he answered, "I promise you, he's been briefed. I spent a lot of time talking with him and all the people around him have explained to him that you've got a dynamic young company, and that you're really going places. I think he's prepared to make a reasonable offer. Please come and sit with the old man and hear him out."

Gordon Greenfield was very persuasive, and I agreed. I got together again with his father, and this time Albert, in the presence of his son, began with a warm speech. He said he wished his son was like me. I thought that was a silly and very embarrassing remark; then, he went on to make some more obscure, rather nonsensical statements. Finally, he came to the point. Since our stock was currently selling at $16, he said magnanimously, he was prepared to give us $8 a share. At that point, I began to laugh and couldn't stop.

"Albert," I said at last, "assuming I was completely bananas and I accepted your quote generous unquote offer, how in the world would you convince the E. J. Korvette stockholders to give you E. J. Korvette at $8 a share?" He replied with an air of complete innocence that if I accepted his offer he was confident of his ability to convince the bankers and our stockholders that they should accept his offer.

I considered this meeting a form of entertainment, and obviously, I still couldn't take Albert Greenfield seriously. We never met with him again. It wasn't a waste of time, however, because while these negotiations, if you could call them that, were going on, we did receive a few favors. On one occasion, Gordon Greenfield provided E. J. Korvette with a fine merchant, Glenn Birnbaum, who made an admirable contribution to the future development of our apparel departments. It was

Gordon, too, who made it possible for us to acquire our downtown Brooklyn location, which to this day is a very profitable store.

By the late fifties, I hadn't been able to consummate any mergers, but we were doing quite well. Our business was on course, our projections were turning out to be accurate, our profits were excellent. It seemed the next step would be to renew acquaintances with the supermarket people from Penn Fruit and with their former competitors in Philadelphia, Food Fair. In the early fifties, Penn Fruit was considered one of the finest food supermarket chains in the United States. It was competing directly with the Food Fair organization, which was centered in Harrisburg and was beginning to forge ahead. Food Fair had acquired a small chain in Florida, which gave them a good base to begin to expand profitably. As a consequence, although Penn Fruit and Food Fair had started out on even terms, the latter was now beginning to do considerably more business.

We had some discussions with Penn Fruit about merging. We wondered if it would make sense, and at the time I thought it would. I was very interested, but their banker was against it and discouraged any kind of association. Consequently, we found ourselves spending more time with the Food Fair people.

If anyone had asked me why we were interested in merging with Food Fair, I would have answered that it was because we were operating in two separate areas. Our beginning had been humble, but we were now moving along on a fast track. If there were any real problems in the merger, they arose from my own psychological makeup. People have called me a perfectionist, but the truth is, I'm much more of a worrier. Like most people, I develop deep anxieties and I have my fears. At the time of our talks with Food Fair I had a tendency to exaggerate the inadequacies of E. J. Korvette. If top management exhibited any shortcomings, I was too timid and negotiated from weakness rather than strength.

I never looked at the positive elements, but always at the negative. For example, if I walked into A&S and examined their men's clothing department, or their men's casual outerwear department, and then compared these with what we had at E. J. Korvette, I got depressed, thinking that we were far inferior.

That was unfair, because our prices were considerably below A&S Although they had such a superior looking department, both aesthetically and from a merchandising point of view, I didn't think about the necessary difference in pricing. The problem was that the brands A&S

was buying were not available to E. J. Korvette, and even if they had been, I'm not sure I would have been satisfied to buy them and agree to maintain the high prices that A&S did. At the time, I had a different feeling about business in general: I believed that the idea was to go out into the marketplace, buy the best merchandise possible for the money, and then sell it as reasonably as you could, related to your cost of doing business. I suppose I didn't have the other point of view because I had come from humble beginnings and had the psychology of a Depression baby. I was a first-generation American, and I didn't have the advantage of being even partially spoiled or seriously secure.

Maybe all this explains why I talked to Food Fair about the possibilities of a merger. From a merchandising point of view, my feeling was that wherever we put an E. J. Korvette store it would be advantageous to have a good supermarket next door to guarantee a certain amount of traffic. By the early 1960s the nation had not yet witnessed the emergence of the great retail shopping centers which would soon dominate the landscape. Department stores were still opening in city areas, but when they opened in suburbia they were isolated, unless they happened to have a few satellite stores around them. Wherever E. J. Korvette went, I wanted to see a good supermarket nearby, with the implied guarantee that our stores would be exposed to a certain amount of traffic every day of the week.

But I had a special interest in Food Fair. It was a rich corporation, and I was sure that if we merged, the result would be increased earnings and net worth for the merged corporation. What I was not considering, to be honest, was the dilution, or potential dilution, that might take place in such a merger. My bankers were aware of it. They were not happy about my discussions with Food Fair, but they stayed in the background because the talks had not yet come to a really serious stage.

We had five separate meetings with the Food Fair people over a period of five years. The first meetings were merely exploratory. I don't think Food Fair took the merger seriously during the first four years of our talks. Our meetings consisted of myself and one or two associates, and two or three representatives of Food Fair. Most of their questions were characterized by a lack of respect, rather than a seeking for knowledge. It's hardly surprising that no agreement was reached.

The Food Fair representative in these meetings was usually Meyer Marcus. He was a sarcastic man who never had anything nice to say. For example, if you were offered a basket of fruit and chose a red apple, he was likely to remark, "Don't you know anything about fruit? White apples are in season this time of year. Why don't you eat a white apple?" Perhaps he didn't mean to be curt and discourteous, but that was the appearance he always gave, and I accepted it as his personality. After our meetings, there was always silence on Marcus's part. He never called back, as was customary, to say something such as, "It was nice talking with you, but we decided negatively," or "We decided to table the matter until next year." It wasn't only E.J. Korvette that received this kind of treatment; that was Food Fair's reputation.

I was surprised, then, after nearly five years of this kind of negotiation, that Meyer Marcus looked me up while vacationing in Florida. He told me the chief executive officer of his company, Samuel Friedland, would like to spend some time with me. I invited Friedland to visit me at the hotel where I was staying with my wife and children, and we spent a comfortable evening together. The meetings that followed were also pleasant and enjoyable in contrast to my sessions with Marcus. I sensed at least some measure of respect from Friedland.

By the early 1960s, the entire E.J. Korvette organization had begun to pull together. We had opened many stores and had taken the volume from roughly $40 million at the time we went public to nearly $400 million. At that time, food markets all over the country were looking into the possibility of going into the department store business.

Food markets are always in a tight squeeze, and they were especially so at this particular time. They had a high cost of doing business, suffered from intense competition and had to deal with a very short markup. Their earnings were always in the range of 1 to 2 percent of sales, occasionally even below 1 percent. It was not hard to understand, in light of these facts, why they thought of branching out into non-food businesses, where conditions were so much better. It was a time when nearly all retailers were enjoying substantial profits, and the food markets believed that by identifying with non-food businesses, they would add a significant dimension to their operations.

Looking back, it seems incredible to me that none of the food chains from California to New York had the presence of mind to go after the viable department store chains seriously. Certainly they had the financial capability to acquire some of the smaller chains, but none of them did. Instead, they turned their acquisition efforts toward discount stores, of a kind I always refer to as one-story, mass merchandising operations. This type of discount operation had already been expanding too quickly, creating stores that were too big and taking on too much nondescript imported merchandise.

E. J. Korvette certainly didn't fit that description at the time, but it seemed clear that Food Fair was following its competition in trying to get into the discount business. When Sam Friedland, accompanied later by Meyer Marcus, began talking with me in Florida, it was with a note of urgency that had not been there before. After our first meeting, it was arranged for us to meet again at Lehman Brothers as soon as I returned to New York the following week.

Before I went to this meeting, I visited Loeb, Rhoades and had a discussion with John Loeb, the head of that house. He urged me not to consider merging with Food Fair. I told him it seemed to me that it would be a good thing for E. J. Korvette, for two reasons. First, we would always have a good food operation linked with us. Secondly, with Food Fair's real estate properties and the more secure financial position that the merger would make possible, E. J. Korvette would be able to grow even faster.

John Loeb still argued against the idea. In his estimation, Food Fair had reached a plateau, and had developed some serious difficulties as far as its profits were concerned. While Food Fair's stock at that time was approximately $32 a share, it was Loeb's opinion that it would be dropping in the years ahead, while E. J. Korvette stock had yet to see its best years. In short, as Loeb said, they needed us more than we needed them.

John Loeb tried as hard as he could to dissuade me from any further meetings, but I had already made up my mind, stubborn and ill-informed as I was. I not only insisted on going to the meeting that had been arranged at Lehman Brothers, but in my heart I knew that I was going to accept the merger. John Loeb was very angry with me, and disappointed. He virtually dismissed me from his office. I went out and met my lawyer, Richard Dicke, and one of his most important partners, Ed Weisl, from Simpson, Thacher and Bartlett. We went over to Lehman Brothers, where we met Louis Stein, the president of Food Fair, Meyer Marcus, who was the merchandise manager, and Herman Kahn, a partner of Lehman Brothers, who was also on the board of directors of Allied Department Stores.

Louis Stein quickly took control of the meeting. He made a detailed comparison of the multiple of earnings of E. J. Korvette and that of Federated Department Stores, asserting that since Federated's multiple was at a particular figure, it was obvious the E. J. Korvette's was too high. Consequently, we should reconsider what our company was worth. Weisl then informed Stein that Food Fair could not buy Federated. The argument went back and forth for a while until I interjected my own plan that I had dreamed up with my wife the night before. I told them frankly I wanted to merge.

At the time of these negotiations, in the early 1960s, E. J. Korvette stock was selling at $16. There were approximately 1,200,000 shares outstanding, of which 400,000 were in my name or my wife's. My offer was simple. My wife and I, representing a third of the stock, would take $10 a share on the merger and give all the other E. J. Korvette stockholders $20 a share. I was willing to do this because at that time I intended to abdicate as chief executive officer, and it was to be my way of showing my appreciation to all the existing stockholders. I wanted to go out a beloved winner.

When I finished making my proposition, Louis Stein looked at me and said, "Gene, that's great. It's a great idea, and that's why we like you. Okay, let's make a deal. We'll give you and your wife $10 a share, and we'll give the E. J. Korvette stockholders $16 a share."

"That's not fair," I told him. "The reason I'm taking the discount is so that the other E. J. Korvette stockholders will get $20."

Somehow that made Stein angry. He stood up and said, "You'll do it my way or we won't do it at all."

"Lou Stein, you ought to be ashamed of yourself," Herman Kahn blurted out. At that point, Stein stormed out of the room.

A few days later, E. J. Korvette stock went from $16 to $20, and during the following week it climbed to $26 a share. I didn't know why that happened. I was busy working in the Philadelphia area. One day when I was in the Springfield store, I had a call from someone who said he was from the banking house of Eastman, Dillon. I picked up the phone at one of the cashier racks, identified myself, and a man who refused to give his name said to me, "I want you to know the following, because I'm so nauseated at the scene that just took place in one of our offices. A person from Food Fair was here, insisting that we put out a negative analyst's letter about E. J. Korvette. When we told him, 'We're not going to put out such a letter,' he said, 'You'll have to, because we made a tremendous blunder about E. J. Korvette, and you will have to put out the letter so we can rectify our mistake.'" Eastman, Dillon still refused to put out the letter, my informant said, and the man from Food Fair had walked out angrily. I asked the man what his name was, but he hung up on me. Before he did, however, he said he felt that he would have been remiss if he hadn't called and told me what had happened, because he was so upset about what Food Fair was attempting to do. I called my lawyer and told him what had happened, and he said, "Gene, forget about it, and forget about Food Fair. Take care of the business."

In the following months, by the end of 1960, E. J. Korvette stock climbed to $160, and during that period, Food Fair stock dropped from approximately $32 to $10. I learned something from all this—the value of a proper relationship between an investment banking house and its client. This is a matter not many business people understand. This was only one example of many, but it made me appreciate how lucky I was to be associated with John Loeb and Loeb, Rhoades. John Loeb had been absolutely right, and I should have listened to him. I got some idea of how much E. J. Korvette was really worth at this time when I was offered $50 million for my stock by Phil Levin, the builder, on behalf of Beneficial Finance—cash on the barrelhead. I turned it down.

There was never again any idea of merging with Food Fair. A few years later, however, I had a call from Meyer Marcus, but it was a changed Marcus. In a very mild and meek manner, he told me he had problems, and wanted to know if he could talk to me about them. "Go ahead," I said. He told me that after our talks had ended, Food Fair had bought what they considered to be a bargain, an organization named J. M. Fields, which had been in bankruptcy. What they had thought was going to be their entry into the retail business proved instead, to be a catastrophe. Fields was now losing $4 million a year, Marcus said, and they didn't know what to do.

This proved to me once again, that food people, no matter how bright they are, never seem to be successful retailers in non-foods. Somehow the combination never works.

When Meyer Marcus asked me if there was anything I could do to help Food Fair, I examined the Fields situation and found that their average store occupied an area of about 60,000 square feet, with minimal service. By and large, a Fields store was a huge, self-service emporium, selling low-priced, cheap merchandise for the whole family, both soft and hard goods. On the basis of my examination, I made a few recommendations to Marcus. Food Fair should hire a strong president for Fields, with an assistant. The president should have the ability to be mobile, to personally get to know every store manager, since each of these men was responsible for all the activities of the store, and to be sales-promotion oriented.

I pointed out to Marcus that what he had to confront was a chain of stores, each of which a very large emporium with no service and a great number of tables loaded with cheap merchandise. What had to be done, obviously, was to fill the stores with people and sell as much as possible. Marcus asked me to recommend someone as president, which I did. The result was that a turnaround occurred, and the stores went from a $4 million deficit to a $9 million pretax earnings figure, under the direction of Bob Reisner, the man I had recommended.

But Food Fair remained true to form. I had done them a good turn for no particular reward, yet I never got a call from them to thank me. In fact, I never knew the figures resulting from Reisner's good work until he told me about them years later. Reisner had been my general merchandise manager before he went to Fields. Eventually, he became associated with Interstate Department Stores.

There is another postscript to the Food Fair story. Years later, I happened to meet Meyer Marcus, and asked him the question that had bothered me for so long.

"Meyer," I said, "tell me, now that we have all these years behind us, why was it that I could never bring off a merger with Food Fair? Please tell me why."

He looked at me a moment and said quietly, "Gene, the reason we never merged with you is because you were so anxious."

It was true. I *was* anxious, always looking for someone to merge with in those days. While it is probably true that the failure to merge was largely my fault, on the other hand, I must consider myself lucky that it never occurred. We did better by ourselves.

I should add that we did considerably better in our own supermarket business. Our philosophy at E. J. Korvette had always been to put as much money as possible in the cash register. Traffic was the name of the game, and we brought in items that would turn over quickly. That was why we started selling fast-moving grocery items such as coffee, tea and catsup. These lead items sold so well that we started to bring in additional food products. Eventually we built a small food department in the stores and did a substantial sales volume with them.

In December, 1953, when we opened our first department store in Westbury, we had a small food section containing about 40 to 50 of the fastest-moving items. The traffic for this merchandise was so great that a year after the store opened, we built a separate food market adjacent to this operation. It was a full-line supermarket with about 10,000 square feet of selling space, which brought the annual sales volume at that location to $6 million. That was the forerunner of our supermarket division, and from then on, when we opened a new department store, we operated a full-line supermarket wherever it was possible.

At least the long, frustrating affair with Food Fair did lead to one fascinating relationship. Louis Stein called me one day from Food Fair, and asked me to do him a favor and meet with someone who had been eager to spend some time with me. This man was Isaac Wolfson, a reputable English merchant who was later knighted. He had just arrived from England, where, in the late 1950s, he was probably the largest catalog retailer in Europe. In England alone, he had at least four separate catalog operations. They were much different from those that were operating in the United States. Salesmen were hired to carry the catalog into people's homes, sit down with them over a cup of tea, and take an order from the family. After the orders were written they were sent in to the catalog house, which in turn employed a separate trucking system also owned by Sir Isaac to deliver the goods. Extensive credit was available for everyone. At one of our meetings, Sir Isaac told me that Great Universal Stores, which represented his interests in the British Empire, earned about $100 million after taxes, which, of course, made it an incredibly successful venture.

Sir Isaac was a portly man, and my first impression of him was that he was also an extremely sharp, adroit, bright individual. Unfortunately, our first encounter was not a social success. He was flippant with me, and I was rather curt with him.

"Why don't you tell me something about yourself?" he began, at our first meeting. I talked for a few minutes about our business, and he asked jokingly, with a half-smile, whether I would consider selling him E. J. Korvette.

Something in his manner made my skin prickle, and I answered, "Under no circumstances will I sell E. J. Korvette."

Obviously, that was not quite true, as I had been negotiating for a merger with almost anyone who would sit down with me. Yet, I heard myself saying, "E. J. Korvette is not for sale. Period."

Our first meeting degenerated into a kind of squabble. From his point of view I feel sure it was good-natured, but from mine, it was another reflection of my lack of experience in dealing with mergers. Plainly, we weren't getting along and I indicated it was time for me to go. I was especially irritated, I think, by something he did during the conversation. His phone was constantly ringing while we talked and instead of having his calls shut off he kept right on answering them. I found this very annoying and discourteous.

As I got up to leave, Sir Isaac remarked, "I don't want you to go away angry. Let me send you a case of Irish whiskey."

"I don't drink," I said.

"Well, that's all right," he said. "Let me send it to you anyway, and why don't you use it to clean your carpets?"

There seemed to be no answer I could give to that, so I said good-bye and departed. It was not what anyone could consider a successful meeting.

Afterward, however, we became quite friendly. On his second visit to the United States, Sir Isaac Wolfson called me, and asked if I would give him a tour of our store on Forty-fifth Street; it was the store that ran through the block. Despite his age and weight, Wolfson kept up with me on the tour; he seemed to be in better shape than I'd thought.

When we finished touring that store, I took him to our suburban store in Brunswick, New Jersey. It was turning out to be an enjoyable day. Sir Isaac's great sense of humor coupled with his Scottish accent made him excellent company. He joked and kidded with our employees in the Brunswick store, and everyone had a fine time.

On the way home, he reopened the subject of whether or not I would consider selling him E. J. Korvette. It was clear that Sir Isaac was most eager to begin a retail business in the United States to go along with the various other interests he already owned here. He was very involved in the wood paneling business, and in other things as well, including real estate. But, he was primarily a retailer, and he was ready to acquire something in that field. Obviously, he had focused his interest on E. J. Korvette.

I knew that he was also interested in Montgomery Ward, and probably had gone as far as to make overtures to that company, but I learned later that he had been unsuccessful there. When he resumed talking about the subject of buying E. J. Korvette, his jocular attitude toward the idea somehow once more made me say no. Perhaps on my part, it was a matter of pride more than anything else. Nevertheless, while Sir Isaac Wolfson was in America, I began to see him socially. On several occasions my wife and I were invited to have dinner with him at the apartment of his nephew, Victor Barnett, a bright young man.

These non-business meetings continued until I had an idea that I thought might bring us to some kind of merger talks, but in a more conservative and experimental way.

"Why don't we start a joint venture in England rather than in the United States?" I proposed to Sir Isaac. "Let's begin in England, see what develops, and then we'll decide on whatever further steps seem best."

We agreed that Sir Isaac would put up $2 million, and that E. J. Korvette would supply our expertise. In short, he would furnish the capital and we would assume total managerial responsibility. The idea was to open E. J. Korvette stores all over Great Britain. Papers were signed, and I made two separate visits to England. We looked at possible locations in London and Manchester, and finally settled on what I thought was a unique opportunity in London. One of the independent department stores had closed its business in a five-story building in the heart of London. The building had five selling floors of about 20,000 square feet each, escalators, elevators and air conditioning. All told, it was an unusual opportunity; no one would expect to find such an ideal situation to start a brand new business. I saw it as the beginning of E. J. Korvette England, Ltd.

To my surprise, however, a third party appeared on the scene, representing a formidable obstacle. After I had recommended that we begin on the London site, Sir Isaac informed me that we would have to get the consent of his only son, Leonard, who today is in charge of the entire Wolfson empire. We went to see him, accompanied by my chief architect, and we discussed the whole situation with him. Leonard Wolfson was adamantly opposed to our beginning in a store as large as 100,000 square feet. He thought we should begin with a smaller enterprise that would demonstrate whether or not our idea had merit.

Naturally, we were very disappointed by Leonard's attitude. Why, after all, should Sir Isaac and I have to begin in a small store just to prove something to this young man? Yet, Sir Isaac, somewhat like George Farkas, was limited in his actions by his legal (or social) relationship with his progeny.

I didn't give up immediately. We looked at other sites, and found another excellent location in London, an interesting building with about 2,000 square feet on each floor. There were five floors and an elevator. It would be, I thought, a rather modest and practical way to begin the kind of business we were considering, which was, in effect, a mini-E. J. Korvette in the heart of London. The idea was to make a study of London and ferret out the departments of merchandise that would be the most exciting to exploit. We didn't intend to compete with the strengths of existing merchants. We planned to introduce a great deal of American-made merchandise. We agreed on the new site, in any event, and when I went back home, I took with me the plans and specifications of the building, so that we could lay it out in terms of an E. J. Korvette store.

We began to exchange correspondence with some of the people in charge of operations in Sir Isaac Wolfson's Great Universal Stores, which made our task easier. Matters seemed to be going along smoothly until one day when I had a call from London. My caller identified himself as Sir Isaac's general merchandise manager, and he began the converstaion: "Mr. Ferkauf, I'm calling on behalf of Sir Isaac, and he implores you not to be too angry with what I have to tell you."

"Don't worry," I said; "I won't get angry. Why don't you come to the point?"

He did. Young Leonard, he said, had decided that the store they intended to give us for the beginning of E. J. Korvette England was making a profit of $19,000, and he wasn't inclined to give it up. When I heard that I forgot my promise, I'm afraid, and smashed the phone down so hard that it broke.

Thus ended whatever possibilities that might have existed for an E. J. Korvette and Great Universal Stores merger. I never had another meeting with Sir Isaac Wolfson. I'm sure he was greatly embarrassed by Leonard's intransigence, and for my part, I had no intention of exposing myself to any further relationship with the young man.

For a man who was so hellbent on a merger, I had compiled at that point, a track record of total failure. The difficulty lay to some extent in my own personality, as I have described it. It also apparently had to do with the unique personality of E. J. Korvette itself. For better or worse, I had created a merchandising operation that couldn't seem to exist comfortably with any other.

4

Running the Stores

HAVING ALREADY GIVEN YOU AN IDEA of how E. J. Korvette was created and expanded, I will now outline the operation of a single store to help you understand the whole process of retailing. A good case history is that of our store in the Springfield district of Philadelphia—the first real department store we opened outside of the New York area in the late 1950s.

The departments which were the most successful in this store are the same ones I will discuss later in this book when I describe the several ways in which people who are starting a new business, or supplementing an existing one, should choose their merchandise.

In terms of volume and actual profit, the most successful department was men's furnishings—ties, dress shirts, sport shirts, underwear, sweaters, slacks, socks and similar items. Men's apparel is not included in this classification. Although the men's furnishings department has always been a great success in E. J. Korvette stores, the failure of the men's clothing department—suits, sports jackets, dress slacks, outerwear such as raincoats and topcoats—has always been an enigma to me. From the time we instituted this department the turnover was slow, and as years went by, it became even slower. Our dollar profits here were always low. I don't think the difference in volume between this department and men's furnishings can be attributed to management personnel, although this might be true occasionally. The real reason, I believe, lies in the fact that the men's furnishings department represents cash-and-carry, impulse sales, and a body of merchandise designed for men but generally purchased for them by women.

Second to men's furnishings, another profitable department in the Springfield store was the combination of hardware and what we in the trade call "patio goods." Hardware is self-explanatory, but "patio goods" represent a seasonal change in the store, reflecting patterns of living in American suburbia. For example, in Spring and Summer the patio area would be occupied with everything needed for the garden and the pool including outdoor furniture. During Fall, the same space would become our Christmas shop.

The significant change that took place in the "patio goods" area, particularly in the early days of the Springfield store, was the tremendous growth in volume and profitability of the automotive department. Today, we don't speak of hardware and patio but of hardware and automotive. Sears, Roebuck developed the best example in worldwide retailing of hardware and automotive goods. It stands as the most effective model for everyone in the business, and in my opinion, it will remain the finest example of departmental development in any retail area.

The third most profitable area was the children's department. There were special reasons for this. There had been a vacuum in practical, decent children's apparel sold at reasonable prices in the Philadelphia area. Customers had to go to department stores which obviously carried the better merchandise. But the problem in buying clothing for children, as every parent knows, is that it is rapidly outgrown. It is also true that people usually buy children's clothing for one season—in some cases the items won't even last that long. Consequently, there is a natural reluctance on the part of a family to spend a great deal of money on expensive children's apparel. Thus, in Philadelphia there was a need for a retailer to offer large assortments of good quality children's apparel at more acceptable prices. We realized that we had filled that need by the amount of business our department did on opening day. For the next ten years, the profits of the children's apparel department were tremendous.

Operationally, this was not an easy department to run. Aside from the need to prod our suppliers constantly and to expedite deliveries directly to the store, the problem of housekeeping was monumental. Fortunately, in the 1950s good help was available and the store's management and the departmental people lent themselves to the difficult task of continually rearranging all this merchandise according to color and size. It was drudge work, but because the children's department was such a success, the employees took pride in the constant flow of merchandise and everyone worked hard.

Following the children's department in sales success was the record department. This was because of our good fortune in acquiring a young man named Dave Rothfeld, who is still with the E. J. Korvette chain. He ran the record department and later was in charge of all our record merchandising, which I believe, represents the largest record sales in the United States.

David Rothfeld came to us from Urania Records—not as a retailer but as a producer. But when he applied for the job he made such an impression on the merchandise manager and me that he was hired the same day. If someone asked me, "Who was the number one merchant you have ever been identified with?" I would have to name Dave Rothfeld.

His department occupied very little space and was located off in a corner of the Springfield store. But from the beginning, he did an exceptional business. He also added an extra dimension to the store by arranging for celebrities in the music world to make visits and autograph records. It added considerably to our prestige and sales.

Still another superb department was housewares. It occupied the store's lower level, a small area of only 3,000 square feet. Yet, it did an amount of business totally out of proportion to its size. On sale days, we could have used an extra 10,000 square feet of space to accommodate the business, and we had a sale at least once a week. The man in charge of housewares as well as small appliances was Murray Beilenson, the first employee I ever hired for E. J. Korvette.

While considering the development of individual parts of the Springfield store, I should certainly not neglect the photo department. Here, once more, we were lucky to have a remarkable young man in charge. I had met Jack Rosenstein while we were both in the Army. At that time, we were in training in the Signal Corps at Camp Crowder, Missouri. Jack achieved instant fame there one day by taking it upon himself to request a meeting with the company captain. He told him that since he had learned all there was to be learned it would be a waste not to send him directly overseas. He had, in fact, been a remarkable student. The captain took him at his word and arranged to have him shipped out immediately.

At the time we opened the Springfield store, Jack was already merchandising for us. Eventually, he became merchandise manager for photos throughout our entire chain of stores. He did an outstanding job. The job was particularly difficult in the late 1950s, because great changes were taking place in the photo industry and many merchandise men fell short of their responsibilities. For example, as new cameras with automatic features were developed, stores that were heavily laden with the old stock had no way of selling it. Jack kept us boldly moving forward; he had the foresight to see what was happening and we were never stuck with obsolete merchandise. He was so efficient in this respect that he helped Macy's dispose of some of their old excess camera stock. His photo department was a big success from the beginning, in both volume and profit dollars, and continued to be so as long as I directed E. J. Korvette.

Just as I would say that Dave Rothfeld was my best merchant, if someone asked me, "Who should have been developed as the next president of E. J. Korvette?" I would have answered, "Jack Rosenstein." Again, it was my fault that this did not happen—an error in judgment. I can now see that Jack should have emerged as president of the company; certainly, no one at E. J. Korvette ever exhibited Jack's innovative ability and tenacity in developing a department.

Most of the departments in the Springfield store were profitable, but others were not, in spite of every effort to push the unsuccessful departments ahead. The major disappointments were men's clothing, ladies' apparel and major appliances. I have already discussed men's clothing, but in the case of women's clothing, one reason we were not successful was, quite simply, people.

When we departed from our original discount concept and got into the department store business, we carried a great deal of what I call "dumb merchandise"—something that's in a box, nationally advertised and generally pre-sold with its ultimate sale to the consumer depending upon price, display and convenience. In the case of ladies' apparel—that is, sportswear, dresses, coats—as our position in the retail community and our reputation became more sophisticated, our importance in the marketplace became more pronounced and more desirable to the vendors.

E. J. Korvette's quality today is, in fact, quite good in both the men's and women's apparel field. Some people have even told me that in ladies' and men's sportswear E.J. Korvette's quality is as good as Alexander's and May's, if not better. I admit it is the kind of observation that warms me. Unfortunately, that was not the case in the years I headed the stores. True, some development of these departments took place. There was a great improvement in stock and in presentation. We spent a lot of money to make that possible but we were not able to achieve proper customer recognition because of the people involved.

"People" began with me. Responsibility must always begin with the man at the top who is in charge of the whole operation. In the beginning we chose people at random to take the merchandising responsibility. Later, we replaced these people with others from competitive stores who were chosen because they had been running a good department elsewhere.

I remember having lunch one day with Joe Weinstein of May's whose store probably had the best ladies' apparel department of its type in New York. At that time, my merchandise manager in soft goods, a capable young man who had previously been with Franklin Simon, had been making constant raids on May's personnel. We had hired so many of their employees that it was becoming embarrassing. Consequently, at lunch that day I said to Joe Weinstein, "I must apologize for taking so many of your people to develop our own apparel business."

"It's okay, Gene," Joe said quickly, "you can take anyone you want. As long as I stay at the store, there'll be no problems."

I was pleased and relieved that he took such a benign attitude toward what was really questionable behavior on our part.

Nevertheless, we were very slow in making the grade in ladies' apparel. It isn't difficult now to see the mistakes we made. For example, I remember a season when we sent our sportswear merchandise manager to Italy and he brought back a quota of sweaters which were distributed to all our stores. We had questioned whether or not he should buy mohair. There was a general feeling that it was no longer important in the market and in the new Fall season its only value would be in low prices. But when the merchandise arrived from Italy, we found to our astonishment that we had an enormous number of mohair sweaters in the low-price range. This might have been fine, but we also had an inordinate number of higher-priced mohair sweaters. These subsequently had to be marked down severely, even before Christmas.

At another time, I bemoaned the fact that our ladies' sportswear people were making another trip to Italy to buy, despite the fact that year after year everything they brought back didn't sell and ultimately led to big markdowns. A transition was taking place in ladies' fashions. The value of Italy as a source for all sorts of knit apparel was diminishing, and the Far East was becoming much more important. Designers there had not only improved the quality of their work as far as detail was concerned, but they had developed the ability to produce merchandise that compared extremely well with Italian goods and cost considerably less. In spite of the transition which was taking place, we seemed oblivious to it at E. J. Korvette.

What we needed to do was examine all the local department stores, find out which ones were doing best in the sportswear department, and pinpoint the people responsible for their success. After that, we should have pirated the merchandiser or buyer responsible, and brought him into the E. J. Korvette organization where we would hope he would duplicate the qualities that had made him so successful in his previous job. That was what we should have done. But, we didn't. Instead, we retained people who simply didn't measure up to what was required and there is no one to blame but myself and my closest associates.

The other difficult and unprofitable department in the Springfield store was major appliances—refrigerators, stoves, washing machines, clothes dryers and so on. Some firms would also include large pieces of brown goods in this category—that is, big consoles or consolettes, combination stereo and television sets and large stereo consolettes.

Major appliances is a particularly difficult area operationally for most department stores, with the exception of Sears, Roebuck. The reason is obvious. You're dealing with heavy merchandise that has to be bought ahead of time, taken to a warehouse, and when it's sold, delivered to the customer. By the time it arrives, it may have a scratch somewhere or the machine may not work and must be replaced. The nature of the merchandise and the cost involved in handling it, make it difficult to cost out this department consistently and profitably.

Another factor is involved. This department is entirely name-brand merchandise, heavily advertised, and extremely competitive, so that the markup has to be quite short. When it's all added up—bulk merchandise involving large trucking and warehousing costs, and the short markup—it's almost impossible to make a profit on this kind of merchandise. There are exceptions, of course. Some major appliance specialty chains deal exclusively with these items and they make profits. But even while I say this, although I know it's true, I can't recall the name of any one chain so I don't believe there can be many successful operations.

Discussion of this subject always comes back to the superb job Sears, Roebuck had done. It is another illustration of what first-rate direction and management teamwork can do for a retail organization. Sears, Roebuck determined at the beginning of their work in this field that rather than buy major appliances from the country's great producers they would develop their own products and their own name. Once they had decided on this course, they pursued it tenaciously. The result is that when a customer goes into Sears, Roebuck to buy a refrigerator or a washing machine, he buys a brand that he identifies only with Sears, Roebuck. After the sale, customer service is also arranged by the company. Because Sears, Roebuck developed its own product, removed itself from dependence on an outside source, and did not directly involve itself in a competitive situation with other stores, it has been able to produce a profitable markup consistent with providing all that is necessary to sell and service such merchandise. This Sears, Roebuck department is so strong and commands such great customer confidence that I can't imagine any other retailer ever overtaking them in this area.

If I were running E. J. Korvette today, my inclination would be to abandon the major appliance department. It would be much too expensive to try to develop anything similar to the Sears, Roebuck operation. There is no assurance that it would even be possible. Besides, a store should not sustain a losing department, not even if the customer expects to find that kind of merchandise in the store.

Such are the things people learn when they attempt to run large department store operations. Sometimes the learning comes too late. In our case, we didn't exactly win the struggle with trying to sell major appliances, but on the other hand, our lack of success didn't materially damage the business. Others have not been as fortunate. In any case, I hope this chapter has demonstrated that there is more to the retail business than simply putting the merchandise out on the shelves and hoping for the best.

5

More Expansion

By the time we opened several more stores in the Philadelphia area, we were already well represented in the metropolitan areas of New Jersey and New York. We had replaced all of our small stores with larger ones and in 1962 we opened the handsome building so familiar to New Yorkers today on Fifth Avenue and Forty-seventh Street.

That was a major move for us. The rent alone on this store was $1 million, yet we had no serious qualms about opening the store, being somewhat secure in the knowledge that within a two-block radius we had four little stores doing a combined $14 million business. The new store only needed to do $19 million annually to break even. Our pretax profit before home office expenses that first year was $3 million; the gross was $30 million. In that 100,000 square feet of selling space, we were doing $300 of volume per square foot.

Next, we began to look toward the Midwest and the South with the idea of expanding. We planned to open four stores simultaneously in the Chicago suburbs; we gave no consideration to opening in any downtown metropolitan area. At the time the Chicago stores opened our plan was to open three other large stores in suburban Detroit. Planning ahead, we thought of the region south of Philadelphia, particularly Baltimore, Maryland, and Northern Virginia—in short, the countryside around Washington, D.C.

This was an ambitious undertaking—a demonstration of how

dramatically our merchandising ideas had changed since we began. No longer did we regard ourselves as a discount store in the sense that we ran a tight ship and were prepared to beat anyone else's prices. Instead, we began to look with covetous eyes on other department stores. In the back of my mind, I nourished the ambition to be identified eventually with stores such as A&S.

There were two directions we could take. We could examine the size of our stores, determine from the stock content which were profitable and which were not, design a store as solid as possible in the departments with which we wanted to be identified, and with due precautions, expand in every direction. That course would have been in keeping with our origins and our accountants were in favor of adopting it.

The other direction, and the one I was drawn to emotionally, would be to make the stores considerably larger than they had been before and design them with the look and splendor and presentation of a conventional department store. My rationale was that the money to be made in retailing had to be made in apparel, fashion merchandise and what I call home decor. By this I mean all the hard and soft goods bought for the home to enhance its appearance. Pictures, for example, are in this category. Having set my sights in this direction, many changes in our old way of doing things were made and new people appeared on the scene who would affect our future development.

One of these people was a young man who had been the number two executive at Alexander's. His name was Jack Schwadron. I had never gotten over my infatuation with Alexander's. My hope for a merger with them was based on the idea (among others) that it would improve our soft goods department, a department in which Alexander's had a much better reputation. Conversely, I had hoped that we could make a valuable contribution to Alexander's' hard goods merchandising. Although the merger never took place, Jack Schwadron represented a kind of back door approach since his family owned about 20 percent of Alexander's. After I met Jack, we quickly came to an understanding whereby E. J. Korvette bought that equity from his family and I asked him to become our merchandise manager.

In making this move, I believed that the presence of someone who had always been involved in the merchandising activities of what I considered to be one of the best soft goods retail establishments would be a positive step forward. I must admit that I also had something else on my mind—the thought of getting 20 percent of Alexander's would prove to be the catalyst whereby a merger would eventually be possible. But the merger never happened. What occurred instead was a lawsuit with Alexander's, a short one which they eventually abandoned at considerable loss. The suit was a federal action, charging us with trying to capture control of the company. In losing this case, Alexander's was compelled to pay us $250,000 and supply us with financial statements twice a year. The mediator's decision urged that the two firms be merged.

Shortly afterward, we bought slightly more than another 23 percent of the firm, not from the founding Farkas family, but from relatives and other stockholders. That gave us a little more than 43 percent interest in the Alexander's department stores as well as their real estate. The total cost of this investment was $9.7 million, stock and cash. About the time I left E. J. Korvette in 1967, this equity was sold for $23.5 million. Consequently, while we never succeeded in merging with Alexander's, in the end our company made a substantial profit from their stock, and this came at a most opportune time.

When Jack Schwadron came to E. J. Korvette as general merchandise manager, we made some changes in personnel as our ambitions in the soft goods field had increased. Jack and I were in complete agreement about the new direction E. J. Korvette was taking, namely, that our stores should take on the physical appearance of a fine department store. We went ahead immediately with our Chicago plans, obtained a bank loan and opened the first four stores there within a period of 30 days. During the same year we opened three more stores in Detroit. But in spite of the fact that our profits were good—we were earning approximately $18 million pretax—all these openings caused a sudden cash shortage. Our cash flow did not provide enough to support the opening of seven big new stores at a cost of about $21 million.

With the help of our attorneys and Loeb, Rhoades, we made overtures to the Prudential Life Insurance Company. Our efforts were rewarded. Before long, we got a long-term loan of $20 million. A year later, Prudential added $10 million more to that sum. That was quite an achievement on the part of everyone concerned and it made E. J. Korvette quite comfortable in its financial commitments.

Thus bolstered, we continued our expansion toward the South. We opened two fine stores in the Baltimore area, subsequently added a third store; opened a large store north of Washington; another in the Maryland countryside; and still another store just south of Washington, D.C. in Falls Church, Virginia.

Sales, however, were proving to be disappointing and our costs of doing business were rising. We had relaxed the customary tight controls we had always exercised. We overhired and overpromoted and that was taking its toll. Sales generally were still quite good, but the ready-to-wear departments were disappointing and these were the areas that should have been making the greatest contribution to our growth. Ironically, most of our earnings were still coming in from the hard goods department. We were running contrary to general form.

In this situation, it's understandable that I began, for the first time, to have doubts about the future. To put it plainly, I was scared. I was concerned most about the fact that earnings had flattened. We were generating the same amount of profit but the return on equity was diminishing, as were our earnings per share. Our ambitions for the apparel departments had not been realized, and I was acutely aware that, while E. J. Korvette appeared formidable and successful to the professional retail community and to our customers, there was still good reason to worry.

The instinct of many retailers in this position would have been to retreat and retrench. Instead, we chose to look for ways in which our business could take on new dimensions and develop fresh sources of revenue.

Our first move was to embark on a door-to-door cosmetic program. The advance planning for this project was excellent. We designed a beautiful catalog, made all the proper arrangements for the merchandise and its packaging and pointed ourselves in a direction we knew was promising. Everyone involved in the planning was confident of our success and there was reason to be because the products were highly satisfactory and the packaging was spectacular.

There was some incidental glamour involved with selecting a name for our line. Initially, we had decided to meet with celebrities and explore the possibility of buying the use of a name from one of them. Our first approach was to Oleg Cassini. We met with him at his Park Avenue apartment and found him to be an affable man who told us some fascinating and amusing stories. He was friendly and interested in the project. After the meeting, we seriously considered using the Cassini name for our product line, but we decided not to hurry and to do a little more prospecting.

Our next approach was to Zsa Zsa Gabor. We sat with her and a contingent of lawyers and managers who were representing her interests. We all had a charming conversation that led nowhere and we departed after a while convinced that a marriage between Oleg Cassini and Zsa Zsa Gabor would be most interesting. As for our product line, we decided to forsake the celebrities and use the name of our own dynamic sales promotion woman, Eve Nelson. Eve permitted us to do it, with the graciousness that characterized everything this wonderful lady did.

Though our planning for this venture had been good, the execution of it turned out to be disastrous. At the end of the first year, the net result was that we had written $2 million in sales, a respectable figure, and there was every indication tht the future would be profitable. On the other hand, we had encountered operational and organizational difficulties which forecast the possibility of huge losses.

The cosmetics had cost a fortune to design, and we had cut back in our hiring of personnel to carry the operation through. The line was managed internally, but it was poorly organized in its follow-through on sales. If a woman ordered a product from our door-to-door salesperson, she had to come into an E. J. Korvette store to pick up the product. Some customers felt it was an imposition.

After we had reviewed the situation, our accounting firm wrote to us suggesting that if we decided to abandon the project then and there, any potential losses could be salvaged by donating the remaining inventories to charity and the net arithmetic would bail us out. I was reluctant to abandon the good work we had done, but I reminded myself that this project was intended to add another dimension to E. J. Korvette and supplement our income. At that point, it was endangering our profitability, so the decision that had to be made was an obvious one. I advised everyone that we would abandon the entire program to avoid suffering any losses.

We weren't entirely through with the cosmetics business, however. There was one more painful but amusing episode to come. As we had developed our transition from small discount stores to spacious promotional department stores, we had begun to entice more glamourous vendors—one of which was Revlon. Charles Revson, the founder and chief executive officer of Revlon, had begun testing his cosmetics in a few E. J. Korvette stores. This ultimately resulted in total chain representation, with the Revlon lines of facial makeup and fragrances amply represented in all of the E. J. Korvette New York stores—with only one exception—the store on Fifth Avenue.

The omission of the Fifth Avenue store, we learned from the Revlon salesman, was the decision of Revson himself, and I was mystified by it. Obviously, the only way to unravel the mystery was to meet Revson and ask him. He was already a somewhat legendary figure, although not unlike many of his successful contemporaries in his obsessive dedication to his business. Revson's obsession, however, approached the fanatical. He consumed executives with a frightening rapidity. When he was convinced that one of them was intellectually exhausted, that person was as good as fired. It was widely accepted that Revson was a tough "sonofabitch" to work for.

My meeting with him took place in Revlon's old headquarters in the Tishman Building on Fifth Avenue. I had been invited for lunch, but no one had told me that Revson was a health food nut who ate very little. I was dismayed when we were served about three tablespoons of tuna fish soaked in oil. My host assured me this was good for my digestion. The luncheon ended with a half-cup of Sanka, while my stomach was still rumbling from lack of food.

In this state of general irritation, I listened to Revson explain why Revlon couldn't allow the sale of its merchandise in our Fifth Avenue store. I knew well enough that it was because the more prestigious Sak's Fifth Avenue store just a few blocks away sold the same line. I wondered how he was going to get around telling me this. Nothing I could have anticipated, however, would have prepared me for the performance Revson gave. Shielding his eyes with one hand, he explained in a subdued and mysterious voice that he had experienced a vision, and in the vision a voice had spoken to him cautioning that Revlon's products should not appear in our Fifth Avenue store because the time had not yet come. When it did come, the visionary voice continued, proper arrangements would be made. With that, he removed his hand and looked at me significantly, as though to say, "Stop knocking me out."

There was no point in having a confrontation with a man who could give me that kind of argument, particularly when he had all the leverage. Besides, I was hungry. The luncheon ended quickly, and I hurried to a nearby restaurant.

Looking in another direction, I began to think about going into the entertainment business. I had long been a devoted follower of the Japanese cinema, particularly the pictures produced by Kurasawa, usually starring Toshiro Mifune. Two of these pictures, in my opinion, were outstanding and I was convinced that with proper attention they could be converted into successful American prototypes.

The first of these films was "The Seven Samurai"—already a tremendous artistic success in the United States; the second was "Yojimbo," which few people had seen at the time, but which I thought had great merit. I decided to ask my colleagues their opinion on buying these two properties from the Japanese, and then start exploring the best way to become involved in converting and producing these two films as an American product. It was my idea to change the location of "The Seven Samurai" to Mexico during the short reign of Maximilian, retain the original story and cast the Mexican film star, Cantinflas, as the ambitious would-be Samurai who eventually became part of the courageous band of warriors. I thought of Jose Ferrer as the aging Samurai who was the leader of the group.

After debating this idea with myself for too long a time, I drafted a letter to the E. J. Korvette corporation in which I guaranteed to assume all the losses from this venture should there be any. I told them I knew it was far afield from the business in which we were engaged, and so I was willing to take on the responsibility to insure that no one would think me careless with the company's money.

My offer was accepted but before I could make a move to carry out my plan, two things happened. A movie producer bought "The Seven Samurai" for Yul Brynner—it later made a fortune as three separate movies. "Yojimbo" was bought by an Italian group which used it to make the first of many "spaghetti westerns" produced in Spain, launching the career of Clint Eastwood who played the lead in this remake entitled "A Fistful of Dollars." It, too, made a fortune in the United States and broke all attendance records in Italy.

Obviously, I'd been right about these two Japanese classics, but was too slow in carrying out my idea. That was the end of our aborted attempt to get into the entertainment business, but even now, I still find myself seriously thinking about how I could involve myself in the movie business. I see this business as an enormously profitable one in the years ahead. The amount of material required to feed home television alone, is staggering. I believe that anyone who becomes involved either in producing or distributing entertainment, is in a position to make great profits.

Though I was blocked off in one direction at the time, there were other dimensions we could add to E. J. Korvette which might be considerably more prosaic. As we expanded into suburbia in the late 1950s, our next ventures were snack bars and beauty salons. The snack bars were part of our main buildings, but they could also be entered from the outside without coming into the store. That arrangement permitted motorists, particularly truck drivers, to come in about eight o'clock in the morning for breakfast. We placed these snack bars in all the larger stores—those in Chicago, Detroit, the Washington, D.C. area (except for Baltimore), and all the stores in the New York metropolitan area.

We were fortunate to hire Artie Kantor, a man who had previous snack bar experience in Florida, to run the snack bars from the beginning. It was a profitable part of the business in all the years we operated them.

The beauty salons came about as a result of the Eve Nelson door-to-door cosmetic program. We believed that one would complement the other. At the time we established Eve Nelson we intended to have salons bearing the same name. In an effort to internationalize the locations and add a certain mystique and prestige to the venture, we went to Milan with the idea of buying an existing salon there.

We enjoyed the four days we spent in Milan, but nothing came of the trip. We didn't find a salon we wanted to buy, but we did meet with the foremost Italian chemical and pharmaceutical firm, Carlo Erba, with the idea of acquiring its products for our stores. Nothing resulted from these conversations either. We came back home and went ahead with our original plan to establish 13 Eve Nelson beauty salons from Chicago to New York. They were well received and enjoyed a good volume, proving to be a decided asset to the stores because of the traffic they generated. By far the most successful of the salons was the one in the Fifth Avenue store, which was busy all day, every day of the week. After I left E. J. Korvette, the firm sold its salons to one of the existing national chains.

Other opportunities presented themselves. While we were establishing our Midwestern stores, we began to examine the possibility of getting into the real estate field. We discussed this at length with our financial advisers who told us that success in real estate ventures would add immeasurably to our cash flow. But in the end, due to our particular tax situation, the net effect would be to reduce our visible profits to the stockholders. Since we were currently enjoying an excellent multiple on our earnings per share, we decided not to tamper with that asset. Consequently, we declined and participated in real estate ventures only as far as the building of E. J. Korvette stores was concerned.

We did, however, make a small exception in Chicago, where without making an investment, we were able to participate in 50 percent of the income from the other establishments in a shopping center where we were building stores. But even here, as time went on, we began to have reservations and made a new arrangement with the developer whereby we backed off as a real estate participant. In exchange the developer paid us $1 million, payable over four years.

The stores we opened in Chicago were modestly successful, but their income couldn't be compared with the stores we had opened earlier. The Chicago-Detroit openings, for example, were not comparable to those in the Philadelphia area; they were profitable, but not as much as we had hoped. Nevertheless, I felt that we were moving in a positive direction, and that the results were reasonably satisfactory. They would have come closer to expectations, I must admit, if I had followed the recommendations of our accountants and made the stores considerably smaller. Their theory was that by making the stores 30 percent smaller, we would decrease our cost of doing business proportionately. Today, there isn't the slightest doubt in my mind that if I had listened, the volume would have been the same and the profits substantially higher. My decision was a mistake, but on the other hand, we had no misgivings about the direction we were taking—which was to be comparable eventually to the typical American department store.

After we had opened the Chicago stores, Montgomery Ward approached us about the possibility of a merger—certainly a switch from earlier days, when I was the one who had sought out other companies. If the offer had come in those days I would have been overjoyed, but now Montgomery Ward was under severe criticism. Their returns were far from satisfactory, the stockholders were disenchanted, and there had been several attempted takeovers. Nevertheless, the very fact that so many others wanted to take over Montgomery Ward was proof that in the financial community it was still considered a desirable plum.

Ed Guterman, their representative who approached us, had previously been a top executive with Sears, Roebuck, and had worked closely with General Robert Wood, the man responsible for the Sears success. It was said that General Wood had passed over Guterman in the selection of a president for Sears, which had impelled him to resign and join the investment banking house of Lehman Brothers, simultaneously becoming a consultant to Montgomery Ward. Presumably, it was Guterman's intention to put Montgomery Ward on a proper path and so demonstrate to General Wood and Sears that they had been wrong in evaluating his ability.

We had several sessions together in which I served as a guide to Guterman in the E. J. Korvette stores. We also spent some time together at his home. Two possibilities emerged from our talks. One was a merger between our two companies, which I wanted very much. The other, which did not appear immediately, was selling our Midwest locations to Montgomery Ward. Apparently, they were preparing an expansion drive under the new leadership and coveted our large Midwest stores. Since Chicago was their home base and our stores there were well located, beautifully designed, and properly sized, they would be a decided asset to Montgomery Ward's expansion moves.

Once again, though in a different way, it seemed I was the biggest obstacle in effecting a merger. My stock position in E. J. Korvette was so substantial that in any company formed as the result of a merger, I would automatically become the largest stockholder. Montgomery Ward was not considering any such possibility. Guterman didn't speak openly about my stock position as an obstacle but since I was so certain that it was, I suggested that in the event of a merger I would consider some other kind of equity for my E. J. Korvette common stock. In any merger undertaking, I was prepared to be part of the team rather than in total control.

But even this compromise was apparently unacceptable. Once again, the merger fell through and I heard no more from Ed Guterman. A year later, there were rumors in Chicago that E.J. Korvette was about to sell its Midwestern stores to Montgomery Ward. When financial reporters asked me if any such sale was being prepared, I emphatically denied it. I was still so chagrined by the failure of the merger that I would never have considered selling our Midwastern stores to them. Besides, the stores were profitable; we were considering opening still more stores in the area and there was no real reason to sell.

In the back of my mind, I must confess, there was also a feeling that as long as Montgomery Ward was so anxious to get our locations, the possibility remained alive that they would get around to talking merger again. I must have overestimated their desire, because nothing ever happened in that direction. I still think such a merger would have been positive in its net results. There were substantial benefits to be derived by both parties, and I believe that if they had been convinced of my willingness to be a part of a team rather than in control, the merger with Montgomery Ward would have taken place.

In spite of the failure of this exciting merger prospect, in the mid-1960s, E. J. Korvette still appeared to the outside world as a vibrant, militant, successful force in the retailing world. But to those of us on the inside, there were problems developing. In retrospect, I'm sure I magnified them; they weren't really that serious. However, things were continuing to change. Our expansion was proceeding at a considerable rate, and we were coming up with splendid locations in the New York metropolitan area. These locations were so valuable that they never again were to be duplicated; they represented great new sources of wealth for E. J. Korvette.

The best of our departments were continuing to thrive and move ahead. By this time, our record and photo departments had achieved national recognition. The disappointments went right on being disappointing. Some of the apparel departments and the major appliance departments were not making any important financial contributions.

It was while the Springfield store in Philadelphia was growing that we began to develop a label, "Spring" products. We registered the name and used it for many of our housware products. From the beginning, the greatest success we had with this label was the development of a washing machine detergent identified as "Spring." We did approximately $500,000 a year in business with this product alone.

One of E. J. Korvette's failings, however, was our inability to nurture our own name in many other areas, and the fault was entirely mine. There was a good deal of developmental work to create private labels within the framework of many E. J. Korvette departments, but this was not done in any organized way. The effort was a superficial one, at best, and by and large, it was left to the imagination and ability of the individual merchandise managers.

What we should have done was set up a management committee that would have been given the responsibility of developing private labels for E. J. Korvette in the most important areas. Eventually, our customers would have thought of these labels as nationally advertised brands. Sears, Roebuck did this admirably, but we did not follow their example. From time to time, my colleagues urged that something should be done in this direction, but nothing happened simply because of my failure to comprehend and assume that responsibility.

One particular part of the E. J. Korvette business which had grown tremendously over the years began having some serious problems in the late 1950s. As I have said, it had been our intention to have supermarkets adjoining, but not inside, our main buildings. The reasons for this were still valid. No retail store creates more traffic than a supermarket, and to have that kind of traffic exposed to the main building every day made the markets a highly valuable asset. At first, these supermarkets had made a profit, and we continued to make a modest income on all our food operations in the New York metropolitan area; consequently, we continued to open them as we expanded.

The operational difficulties began with the markets we opened outside the metropolitan area. Problems arose from our methods of handling food. For example, we differed from conventional food chains in that we did not have a distribution center. Instead, the food stores were designed to be 20,000 square feet, with 15,000 feet of front space devoted to selling, and the back portion approximating the receiving and distribution areas of a commercial supermarket chain store. This worked out well in the case of canned goods, groceries and all the basic package staples where our volume was astronomical. At the time we probably had the largest volume per square foot of any supermarket chain for our size.

Unfortunately, when we went to Chicago, Detroit, Baltimore and even as close as New Jersey, our method didn't work. It might have if people had been absolutely dependable. Every manager we hired for our food markets was given the buying responsibility for perishables— that is, meats, produce and so on—and the authority was usually passed on to the merchandisers immediately under him. If we could have relied on the integrity and ability of these men, to the extent we had on those in the New York area, our food operations probably would never have gotten into trouble.

But people who had been thrust quickly into important roles of buying and merchandising could not cope with the situation, and the end result was that the quality of our perishable foods outside the New York metropolitan area was poor. That led to a large volume in the low-margin canned goods department and no volume at all, regardless of margin, in perishable goods. At the end of one particular year, we found that we had losses of about $1 million directly attributable to the poor performance of the out-of-town supermarkets.

Something had to be done about this. From the beginning, our basic philosophy was that the E. J. Korvette stores were our reason for being in business and all other dimensions could only be tolerated to the extent that they made a contribution. If they turned out to be liabilities, some other solution would have to be found. As far as the markets were concerned, the answer was surgery. We sold the Detroit, Chicago and Southern markets to food chains. The experience had such a demoralizing effect on the stores, however, that we decided to find a food chain with which we could merge. We recognized that we needed professionalism as well as proper distribution facilities and that merger with experts would be beneficial to everyone.

We found that there were two supermarket chains in the New York metropolitan area that geographically worked out well in relation to the locations of our markets. Ours were very desirable properties, as they were new and extremely well turned out. The decor had been designed by department store people. If we had chosen to sell the markets by themselves, there would have been no problem. The chains would have lined up and started bidding for the privilege of buying them.

But that wasn't what we wanted. We wanted to find a solid, substantial, well-merchandised food chain that geographically coincided with our markets. This would be the basis for a merger. The two chains that filled our specifications were Supermarkets General, a New Jersey-based operation, and Hills, a small chain on Long Island. Supermarkets General had its origin in several small supermarkets whose owners were a friendly group, hoping to improve their lot by merging their stores and their efforts. They were buying jointly from this cooperative, and like all the other supermarkets in New Jersey who were buying from it, used the trade name of Shoprite. While they were still using that name, however, they went public, and were listed on the New York Stock Exchange as Supermarkets General.

It was this chain, rather than Hills, that really met our needs, and a meeting with their executives was arranged. The conference to discuss the possibility of a merger was to take place in our offices. What we didn't know was that they were thinking of how great it would be for them to be identified with E. J. Korvette by taking over the running of our supermarkets, and at the same time have the advantage of our expertise in non-foods. With these two concurring objectives, we met.

As we sat around the table, I remarked casually to Herb Brody, one of their executives, "Would it make sense for E. J. Korvette to merge with Shoprite?"

I had intended to make the remark simply to start the conversation, but Brody thought I meant that E. J. Korvette wanted to merge with the cooperative in New Jersey because their corporate name was Supermarkets General and Shoprite was only the name they used on the stores. He was so disappointed with his interpretation, that he blurted out, "Shoprite will never merge with anybody."

What he meant was that the cooperative wouldn't merge with anyone, but I, in turn, misunderstood him completely, and took his statement to mean the the merger we had been contemplating was not possible. At that point, I lost interest and shortly excused myself and left the room. Incredibly, it was this simple misunderstanding that ended a merger which would unquestionably have taken place between E. J. Korvette and Supermarkets General. Years later, after I retired from E. J. Korvette, Brody and I became friendly. At the last lunch we had together, the conversation was about our past associations. Both of us suddenly realized what had happened—Herb's disappointment was so great at that moment, I thought I saw tears in his eyes. I, too, felt like crying.

This failure had an unfortunate result. In 1964, we merged with Hills instead, and from the inception of that deal, there was never any degree of working compatibility between the executives of the two companies.

It was particularly hard for me to reconcile myself to the failure of our merger with Supermarkets General as I watched their progress in later years. They became one of the best food merchants in the United States, now known as Pathmark. By virtue of their own merit and industry, they not only developed a great food chain throughout the New York area, and into New Jersey and Philadelphia, but more importantly, they won for themselves a great deal of prestige in the eyes of consumers. Their reputation was, and is, admirable. I think it is well deserved. Their stores are large and spacious, and they are merchandised magnificently. Recently I visited a store in the Bronx, and I

can honestly say, it was the best-looking, best-merchandised food
supermarket I've ever seen.

Once they had made their decision to expand, Supermarkets General moved in their characteristically energetic way and acquired a
large number of non-food department stores, catalog chains and do-it-
yourself stores—all sorts of diverse retail situations. It is no secret by
now that most of these acquisitions proved to be dismal failures. Today,
as far as I know, they still have a superb and very profitable food business, but the problems that have developed in their non-food enterprises have unfortunately been swallowing up the profitability of the
food chain.

If we had accomplished our merger with Supermarkets General,
I'm sure E. J. Korvette would have successfully remained in the food
business. The overall result might have been spectacular. The merger
with General might also have forestalled, or at least postponed indefi-
nitely, my retirement from E. J. Korvette. When we turned to our
alternative, the Hills Supermarkets, it was the beginning of the end for
me. These stores were generally small in size, located in Queens, Nas-
sau and Suffolk counties, and they seemed to fit in nicely with our
geographic pattern. They had just completed an aesthetically interesting and at the same time practical food distribution center; the way
they appeared on paper was very encouraging. Through Loeb, Rhoades,
the merger was accomplished—the first merger I ever made. There was
no reason why it should not have been successful. All the factors
involved indicated no difficulties, and the results should have been
favorable. However, we found that as time went on it was absolutely
impossible to work with the people at Hills in a way that would have
been in the best interests of the corporation.

Eventually, our inability to work together led to the dismissal of
some of the Hills people, and ultimately resulted in my own retirement. In 1968, E. J. Korvette sold the entire food chain, including both
Hills and E. J. Korvette food stores, to Pueblo Supermarkets for $26.5
million. This occurred at the same time as the sale of E. J. Korvette's
stock in Alexander's, with the result that E. J. Korvette ended up
about $50 million richer.

As early as 1966, I began to realize that our 25 percent markup,
with a cost of doing business at 23 percent, was too close for comfort.
We were still encountering difficulties in stocking elite brands of wearing apparel at discounted prices. Raising the markup would only dissi-
pate the volume. I was constantly puzzled about what to do. One possible solution was to go into quality private labels with respect to hard
and soft goods, *a la* Sears, Roebuck.

Realizing even more importantly that I was too tired—mentally and physically—to undergo such a complete change, I began to look for a personality to take E. J. Korvette in that direction. In 1966, I met with Charles Bassine, the successful and dynamic head of Spartan Industries, which operated roughly 60 discount stores under the name of Spartan Atlantic. This led me to my final merger.

At the time of the merger between Spartan Industries and E. J. Korvette, in 1966, the net worth of all 40 E. J. Korvette department stores was $150 million, of which approximately $50 million was cash. All of my stock was then sold to mutual funds through Simpson, Thacher and Bartlett. I deferred completely to Charles Bassine, and in 1968, retired.

What is there to learn from all this: one primary lesson, people make a business. In any given retail situation, if you have the best of everything that is available in terms of location, building, merchandise and all else that goes to make a fine retail store but the people involved are not capable of working together as a team, the venture is certain to fail. There is one important thing to remember in starting a business whether it's done alone or with a partner and whether it's a stationery store, a corner candy store or a department store: you must have a close rapport with those with whom you're going to spend all your working hours. Compatibility provides a decided, and perhaps even decisive, advantage. At the very least, it will improve your chances of success. If you don't get along with your partner or with your colleagues, not only will the business suffer, but you won't enjoy what you're doing and in the end the endeavor won't be worth the effort.

As you've seen so far in these pages, the problems of retailing are numerous and difficult. Nevertheless, anyone can start a retail business in this country if he or she knows how. And, it is the "how" I'm going to talk about in the chapters that follow.

KORVETTE'S
EUGENE FERKAUF

Time Magazine, *July 6, 1962...."Today he (Ferkauf) rules a fastgrowing retailing empire that consists of 17 stores in the Northeastern area between Hartford, Conn. and Harrisburg, Pa. In the past nine months alone, Korvette's profits have risen 18% to $4,268,000, and the company's sales in fiscal 1962 will amount to $230 million. All this Ferkauf has accomplished by pursuing a business philosophy that is as old as the Industrial Revolution: discard costly frills, use low prices to lure customers and make up for low profit margins with high volume...By succeeding at it in the sluggish 1960s, Eugene Ferkauf has seized the lead in a retailing revolution that is shaking up every U.S. merchant from Main Street to Manhattan's Fifth Avenue."*

Volume 1, No. 8   April, 1961

EJ's EUGENE FERKAUF FEATURED IN TIME MAGAZINE

TIME MAGAZINE in it's March 16th issue, featured an exciting article on the dynamic growth of E. J. KORVETTE, INC. and its founder, EUGENE FERKAUF. Although we are honored with this tribute to our ever growing organization, it must be pointed out that the editor of a magazine is only interested in relating to his readers as much information as it is possible to include in a limited amount of space. As a result, the individual employee may not have been credited with his just due, in that article.

BUSINESS WEEK

February 10, 1962

Fifty cents
A McGraw-Hill Publication

How stock options actually work
Management

Below: Korvette's Eugene Ferkauf pits his brand of discount selling against the carriage-trade tradition of Fifth Avenue [Page 72]

Business Week, *February 10, 1962...."Ferkauf still puts in 10 or 12 hours a day six days a week. And he thinks about the company on Sundays..."*

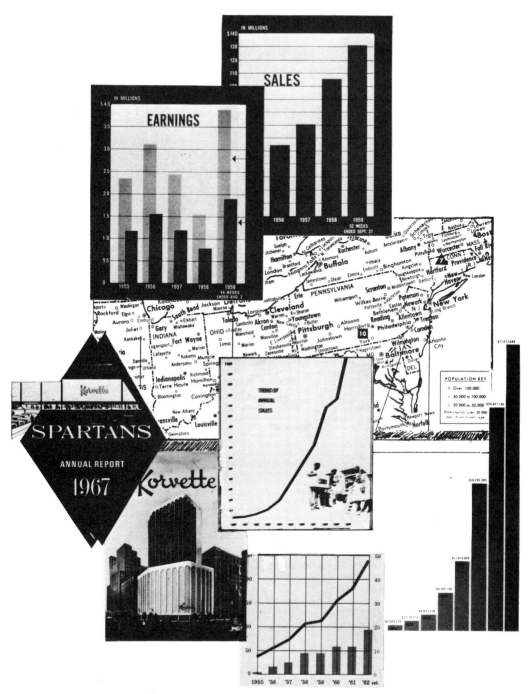

When he sold out his investment in the E. J. Korvette stores in 1968, Ferkauf himself netted $28 million from his initial investment of $4000 twenty years earlier. The company's history was impressive: at the time of incorporation in 1955, E. J. Korvette total sales amounted to over $36 million. By 1962, the figure climbed to $180 million; in 1968, when the company was sold to Spartan Industries, total sales amounted to over $800 million.

In 1948, Eugene Ferkauf (left) opened the first E. J. Korvette store with a $4000 initial investment. The stock included small appliances and jewelry in addition to fine luggage. E. J. Korvette first employees were George Yelen (center) and Joe Zwillenberg (right).

DISCOUNT PAYOFF

In 1954, Eugene Ferkauf (left), was about to open his sixth Korvette store—on Manhattan's West 48th Street. But he found he couldn't finance it himself. "We passed the hat," he reminisces. About 100 employees dug up $150,000—enough to swing the deal. In the first year, they earned 30 per cent on their money.

When Ferkauf began opening branches and annexes of E. J. Korvettes, to fill the staff he hired old school friends. A photograph of Ferkauf's graduating class at Tilden High in Brooklyn looked like the Korvette executive roster.

KNOW ALL MEN BY THESE PRESENTS, that we, the undersigned, having heretofore contributed to a common fund deposited with JOSEPH ZWILLENBERG in accordance with a certain written instrument dated Sept. 15, 1953 executed by us, do hereby acknowledge, certify and declare that the said JOSEPH ZWILLENBERG, at our instance and request, has applied the said funds to the purchase for us and in our behalf of certain shares of the capital stock of KORVETTE-48TH ST. INC., a New York corporation, and of certain bonds issued by said corporation, proportionately to the amounts of our respective contributions to said fund; and we do hereby ratify and affirm the said application by said JOSEPH ZWILLENBERG of said monies to and for said purpose and we do further ratify and affirm all that the said JOSEPH ZWILLENBERG has done and performed with said funds for us and in our behalf; and we do hereby release and discharge him of any and all liability and responsibility in connection with said funds and said purchase of said shares and bonds and of and from any and all claims and causes of action which we and each of us may have had or now have or may hereafter have at any time heretofore to the day of the date of these presents.

IN WITNESS WHEREOF we have hereunto subscribed our names this 17 day of May, 1954.

NEW YORK STOCK EXCHANGE
ELEVEN WALL STREET
NEW YORK 5, N.Y.

DEPARTMENT OF STOCK LIST
PHILLIP L. WEST
    DIRECTOR
ARTHUR L. RAUCH
    ASSISTANT DIRECTOR
LOUIS J. HASSELBACH
    ASSISTANT DIRECTOR

February 18, 1957

Mr. William Willensky, President
E. J. Korvette, Inc.
12 E. 46th Street
New York 17, New York

Dear Mr. Willensky:

I am pleased to confirm that the Common Stock,
$1 par value, of E. J. Korvette, Inc. was admitted to
the list and to dealings on the New York Stock Exchange
at the opening of the trading session today. Registration of the Common Stock under the Securities Exchange
Act of 1934 was declared effective by order of the
Securities and Exchange Commission, dated February 13,
1957.

Very truly yours,

Arthur L. Rauch
Assistant Director

HEG:fr

cc: Mr. Richard N. Dicke
    Simpson, Thacher & Bartlett

— OWN YOUR SHARE OF AMERICAN BUSINESS —

E. J. Korvettes retained characteristics typical of a conventional discount house—low overhead, high turnover and no frills. Customers flocked to the stores enabling the company to go public in early 1957, showing total sales of $70 million.

A meeting of the board included from left to right Bernard Waltzer, assistant treasurer, Richard Weil, former president of Macy's, and Stanley Grant, partner of Loeb, Rhoades, and Ferkauf.

How To Start
Your Own Retail Business

6

You, Too, Can Succeed in Retailing

IN CREATING A MULTIMILLION DOLLAR FINANCIAL EMPIRE from a $4000 start, I did something that was, of course, unusual. I would not want you to think that anyone else with the same amount of beginning capital can hope to achieve the same success simply by reading the advice I'm going to give in the pages that follow, or perhaps by any other means. One of my competitors once called what I did a fluke, and I never disagreed with him.

On the other hand, I think my story does testify to the fact that in America, given a small amount of money and a sincere desire to begin a business, there is a good possibility of achieving some measure of success.

Starting Out

Years ago if anyone had said to me, "Gene, do you think someone can start a business with $4000?" I would certainly have said yes. But recently I was looking around out of curiosity to see what the possibilities might be for starting a business now, and I found to my dismay that the opportunities were no longer as ripe and ready for the plucking as they used to be. I discovered that in most cases the amount of money required to start what I considered a modest business was somewhere between $100,000 and $250,000.

Nevertheless, I'm still convinced that it's possible to begin, add to or supplement some form of retail business with a very modest investment. However, it takes close attention to some fundamentals and requires sensible decisions. If you add up how much rent you'll have to pay, how much the fixtures are going to cost and other fixed expenses, you may find that you're not financially equipped to go into business. In that case, abandon the idea. But if these factors are in balance, there is no reason to hold back; in fact, the troublesome factors themselves may be altered. By starting in a small town instead of a large one, for instance, the rent commitment is lowered, or perhaps it will be possible to rent part of a store, in conjunction with another business. Fixtures, too, can represent a modest investment if you're willing to settle for simplicity. Remember that in cities, everything is going to be more expensive. And if you can afford only a modest investment, you must be willing to start at the bottom.

Let's take a simple example. Here is Mary Jones, who is already running a greeting card shop in a small town. (She rents the store and she works there all day.) It's a gentle business, and from it she derives a modest income. What can she do to supplement it? She is intelligent and industrious. If you asked her, I'm sure she would agree that it would be marvelous if there was something she could do to help pass the time more pleasantly and profitably.

In Mary's case, I would recommend that she add certain classifications of nationally advertised housewares to a part of her store. Specifically, she could go to a local distributor (I'll explain exactly how to do that later) and buy the best-selling components of the Corningware line. It's a highly successful housewares line, familiar to everyone, nationally advertised therefore presold, and always in demand. To buy it, Mary could set aside a small amount of money, as little as a thousand dollars, or even less. With this much capital, she could go to the distributor, and working with him, select for her store in limited quantities the best-selling parts of the Corningware line. She would buy individual pieces and the sets as well. In addition, she should also buy, again in small quantities, the Corningware line of dishes known as Corelle.

The distributor will give her the catalog, a glowing brochure in full color, and in it she will see all the electrical appliances made by Corningware. These appliances are beautiful, well constructed and they work well, but they're in short demand compared with the housewares. So she will settle for housewares, and when they arrive, she will display them as artistically as possible in a part of her store where they will be readily seen. If someone should inquire about the electrical appliances, she will have the catalog and will be able to write orders without having to stock them. Few sales will be lost that way.

Mary should visit the local department stores and see how they display the merchandise she's selling. Using her own good taste, she will be able to do as well if not better for herself. As for pricing, I would recommend initially that she work on about a 15 percent markup over cost on the Corningware sets, at 20 percent over cost on the individual pieces and at 15 percent over cost on the sets of Corelle dishes. To the extent that she sticks to these short markups, she will build a reputation for being competitive. Certainly she will be selling much cheaper than any of the local department stores.

If she gets special orders from the catalog, especially the appliances, she should work on 10 percent over cost because she will not have the merchandise on hand and will have to order it specially for the customer, who has no choice but to wait for the special order, since he is getting it at such a low price.

This formula can be applied to any other kind of store, whether it's jewelry, piece goods or whatever. (There are exceptions, of course—like tire stores, which are complicated enterprises where investment in stock is large, and equipment and service costs are high.) It's a simple way to supplement an existing business in a modest way without any exposure. Why do I say "without exposure?" Because the merchandise I'm describing and recommending here is nationally advertised. It's important to keep that in mind. At E. J. Korvette, we always obeyed the rule never to let ourselves be tempted by unadvertised, unidentifiable merchandise. By selling nationally famous presold merchandise only, you will avoid markdowns and excessive customer returns. As for the problem of prices and inflation, the odds are that if the merchandise is selling slowly, the cost price will be going up from time to time, as it has been during the past few years. Consequently, the program I have just described is the most conservative route for anyone who wants to get into retailing.

Distribution

The next problem is distribution. In the United States, there are intermediaries, or distributors, for famous, brand-name merchandise, all organized in various classifications. For example, in the general classification of housewares, there are Corningware, Farberware, Revereware, Pyrex, Wearever and many other brands of pots and pans and kitchen utensils, including aluminum cookware and the plastic items needed in the refrigerator. Another large classification is chemicals, which includes the detergents, bleaches, deodorants and other cleaning agents to be used in the house. But this is really a sub-classification under housewares, so when we're dealing with that category, we should realize its huge proportions.

To distribute these and other goods, there are a great many distribution centers, both in and outside of the big cities, which employ salespersons who visit stores in every part of the country. These centers are stocked with a wide variety of merchandise: housewares, health and beauty aids, cosmetics, hardware, automotive equipment, small appliances, radios, television sets, cassettes, tape recorders, records, tapes. There are also many other nationally advertised, presold items that you might want to carry in your retail store: Timex watches, Rockwell and Texas Instrument calculators, famous brands of pantyhose, a line of men's socks. But remember, in dealing with these items, stick to the name brands, be firm and positive about the character, quality and identification of the merchandise you're going to buy and sell.

In making these recommendations, I'm conscious that I didn't follow my own advice when I started out. E. J. Korvette began, you'll remember, with luggage and leather goods, and some famous brand small appliances as an accommodation—but I wouldn't recommend that stock mix today because luggage moves too slowly. That industry has gone through dramatic changes twice in my lifetime. When I was a small boy, its importance lay in big, bulky, heavy trunks because people traveling overseas went by ship. If you bought a piece of luggage in those days, you took either a heavy trunk or something in leather. Any piece of luggage considered respectable had to be in leather, and the quality of the leather, plus the bag or trunk's workmanship, determined the price.

Changes took place in this pattern during the Depression, and then the rise of air travel caused a revolution in the field. Heavy trunks were eliminated and heavy leather cases were replaced by well-made, lightweight airplane luggage. Even so, today I look askance at luggage as a vehicle to launch a new business. You simply can't sell enough luggage. In families, it is still very much a hand-me-down item, so that the industry itself remains a rather modest one. I say this even in the face of luggage's recent popularity. If you don't believe it, ask yourself how often *you* buy luggage. However, if a luggage store is also selling handbags, leather goods and similar items, it is still possible to be successful.

The Student

I have been talking so far about only one of many possible situations in starting a business. I am going to give you some rather oversimplified examples of other possibilities, and from them I think the reader may be able to determine how and to what extent they can be applied to his own circumstances, or possibly suggest others to him or her.

College students, for example, are potential retailers while they are still in school. Many are financially struggling to stay there. A typical student in these circumstances, for example, may be eating only one meal a day, and faces a constant battle to make ends meet. How could such a young man do anything about starting a retail business while he's having such problems?

It's not as hopeless a situation as it appears. Assuming that his university has an engineering school, one of the things he could do is to get a catalog describing calculators, preferably from one of the major companies—Texas Instruments, Rockwell, Casio, Hewlett-Packard or Sharp. With the aid of the catalog to inform him about what his cost prices are going to be, he could begin his career by selling to his fellow students while he is still in school. One of the largest selling calculators in American engineering schools is a scientific unit which retails for $79.95 in virtually every department store. But, the student can buy this calculator for much less, with enough leeway for him to offer large savings to the other students and at the same time make a profit for himself. If he sold any combination of ten calculators a week at the school, he could not only effect savings for the students' but make $50 a week for himself.

Calculators are an obvious item, but it could just as well be toaster ovens. Not long ago, just before the colleges opened in the Fall, I was amazed to learn of what seemed to me an incredible number of toaster ovens bought by parents for children who were going away to universities. These ovens are likely to be available at a distributor who is probably not far away from the University.

For the working student who wants to earn extra money by starting his own business in college, there are a number of items available besides calculators and toaster ovens. His business could be in radios, tape recorders, records, cassette players, cassettes. The initial move is to find out what is in demand at his particular institution, and then he can become the intermediary between the desired merchandise and that community.

(At the end of this book I have included a list of distributors of appliances, calculators, health and beauty aids, cosmetics and a good many other classifications. Though far from complete, the list is a large one.)

The Factory Worker

But now, let's take an entirely different locale. Here is a man who works in a factory; it could be anywhere in the United States. He is looking for some kind of supplemental income. What are the pos-

sibilities for him? As a factory worker, the chances are that he and his
fellow workers are the kind of people who do things themselves—make
their own repairs around the house and fix their own automobiles.
That means our worker, Joe Brown, already spends some of his spare
time at various distributors. To go into his own business, he could start
with power tools, acquiring from the nearest distributor catalogs from
such well-known firms as Black & Decker, Rockwell and Stanley. He
will have no trouble getting wholesale price sheets for this merchandise from the distributor.

At that point, Joe Brown is in business. He now represents the full
line of power tools by Black & Decker and Rockwell, as well as the
highly popular line of hand tools by Stanley. He has all the catalogs,
the pictures, specifications of the merchandise and the wholesale price
sheets. All that remains is for him to make this knowledge available to
his co-workers in the factory.

Let's say Joe does this for a year or so, and finds himself in the
month of December selling a great amount of merchandise. At that
point, it's not unlikely that a close friend or relative will come in to
help him, and they soon find the income they're getting from this work
is larger than their salaries. That might lead them to make the big
break—to leave their jobs and possibly work out of their homes, or in a
garage, or maybe even in a low-priced store somewhere near the factory.

The wheels are turning by this time. Joe and company have established a reputation for selling good hardware, and they have a following. People know who they are. Besides this personal relationship,
there is the fact that they will sell more reasonably than the conventional department or hardware store. As business increases and they
turn over their stock of products, they begin to diversify and carry a
larger assortment of hardware items. Then they elect to carry the
best-selling automobile items currently in demand.

Assume that another year goes by, during which Joe Brown and
his helper-partner are very busy. The chances are that they will make
another decision—to move into larger quarters. If they are wise, they
will still be carefully concerned about the rent, still operate under
modest conditions and understand that they are going to keep on working hard. But as soon as they have larger quarters and an increased
following, they find that they have built up such credibility with the
distributor that he is now willing to extend reasonable credit terms to
them. That encourages them to expand into housewares. Now, besides
their hardware and automotive business, they have a housewares line
which will include chemicals for the home. The probability is that their
sales will increase and their stock turnover will do the same.

What has happened, obviously, is that Joe and his partner have added new dimensions to their business. And finding themselves successful with housewares and chemicals, their next step is to go into small appliances, including the whole range of nationally advertised G.E. toaster ovens and steam irons, Oster blenders, Hoover vacuum cleaners and the electrical hair-care products that have become so popular in the past few years.

By this time, it's likely that the partners will realize that they need still larger quarters, and when they get them, they will be able to take on a complete line of G.E. radios, portable television sets, cassette players, recorders, packaged stereo sets and similar items. I have mentioned General Electric here and elsewhere simply because it is the largest selling line in the United States and represents the best value in the low-priced field.

Joe and his partner can continue to build their business in the sound-and-sight category by adding Sony or Panasonic lines, similar to General Electric's products in some respects, but in a higher price range, so that customers who are willing to pay more can be satisfied.

Expanding Your Business

What I have described are the humble beginnings of a small business, and how it continues to grow. In time, the partners will have the beginnings of a department store, if that is what they want. The whole process is certainly not unusual. All the great department stores and variety chains in America started from just such small beginnings, and sometimes even smaller than the examples I've described. Many a department store began with the first generation uncle selling his merchandise from the back of a mule. Some of our most famous specialty stores have similar shoestring origins. It's necessary to start *somewhere,* and if you cast yourself as a pioneer, the beginning is going to be humble.

There are those who never rise much above that level, of course, who make a living and are satisfied after their own fashion—or if not satisfied, at least reconciled to what they have. But there are others who, by virtue of initiative, drive, intelligence, luck—and believe me, luck is important—will take off from their small beginnings and grow into something big. Many retailers arrive at the crossroads in their lives where they have developed an important business in their towns. It provides them a comfortable livelihood with enough money to enjoy vacations or take up just about any pursuit they fancy. Such people can say to themselves, "I have created this business as a retail distributor in my town, and it's supporting my life style in a way that satisfies me."

Two options are open to this man. He can be content with the success he has achieved, spend his time keeping it at an even level and enjoy himself in the kind of life he has. Or he can say to himself one day, "This business is functioning; it's on the way. But I've got some terrific help [from a wife, a relative, or a good friend] and I'm going to open another store. And if that turns out to be successful, I'm going to open a third store."

If he is torn between these options, he can't walk around the corner and ask his friend, or a lawyer, or an accountant, or anybody else what to do. The answer, plainly, lies within himself. Only he can make the decision. If he's the kind of man who wants to shoot for the moon, nobody will be able to dissuade him and he will go as far as he can. If, on the other hand, he's the kind of man who has arrived at a point in life where he's satisfied with his luck, he will pull in the reins and take care of what he has achieved to that point.

Obviously, I'm for the man who wants to shoot for the moon, since I'm that kind of individual myself. There are so many opportunities waiting. Every time I think about E. J. Korvette's record business, which is running in the area of $50 million now, I wonder why more people don't take up this particular kind of retailing. Although it's true that the company's great success is due to the dynamism of the man in charge, records are a good business with which to start out. However, they initially require more money than health and beauty aids, cosmetics, housewares, hardware, automotive goods, small appliances or the other classifications I've mentioned. In addition, they do require a retail store; you can't begin such a business in your home or garage. So much of record selling depends on impulse buying. Many people do go to buy records knowing specifically what they want; they buy an album and that's it. But I would venture to say that at least 50 percent of all the records, tapes and cassettes sold in the United States are sold by exposure.

However, you don't need a whole store for records. It can be part of a store. You could approach someone who is operating a gift shop, or a greeting card store, and make a deal by which you would rent a corner of the shop to set up a modest record department. This is the kind of beginning that takes only a small amount of money, and by "small" I mean that with no more than $5000 in hand it is possible to begin such a record shop. It's understood, of course, that the shop will sell more than records. Cassettes, tapes and auxiliary items that complement them will certainly be on your shelves, and possibly related items like needles and record cleaners.

Developments in the field of electronic entertainment portend new and greater profits in this field. For some time now several major corporations in various parts of the world have been developing devices to play through home television sets in a manner similar to audio cassettes or records. Whether these visual signals are going to come from video cassettes or video records, or both, is still not certain, but both are now technologically possible.

Some have compared this development to the advent of the long-playing record, and predict that its results will be as revolutionary. The possibilities are exciting, and from the retailer's point of view, open up endless vistas of selling. In the near future, it appears, people will be able to go into a record store and buy either cassettes or discs containing old and new motion pictures, sports events of the past, instruction of every kind (the teaching possibilities are already being exploited), full-length plays and operas, even hard-core pornographic movies—no one will be neglected, since these devices will encompass everything now available in other entertainment media. Clearly, this is going to become a major part of the home entertainment business. It will take mass production by the big companies to bring prices down, just as it did in television, and those companies will have to take some losses until the mass market is developed. But eventually it will happen, and more fortunes will be made in retailing as well as in manufacturing.

When this occurs, record stores, which presumably will be the primary source for the new devices, are going to do a tremendous business in video cassettes and/or discs. No one really knows yet what this may do to other parts of the entertainment business, but the history of technology shows that competing technologies seldom cancel each other out. The print media, for example, have successfully faced the competition of bicycles, automobiles, motion pictures, radio and television, all of which were prophesied to mean their doom, but more magazines, books and newspapers are being sold today than ever before. Similarly, visual entertainment at home which can be bought easily and cheaply in a store may hurt movie and other theatres to some extent, but there is no proof that people's living patterns will change so radically that they will not look for amusement outside the home. It was freely predicted in 1939, when the first public telecast was made, that television would produce this result, but obviously it has not.

Nevertheless, I feel strongly that anyone who goes into retailing today with a small record shop is getting into a business that is not only highly profitable as matters stand, but will take on substantial new dimensions as home video entertainment progresses.

The Opportunities

To sum up: For the individual who wants to get into retailing today, the national scene is full of opportunity. Merchandise such as health and beauty aids and cosmetics, housewares and small appliances, hardware and automotive products, radios, portable television sets, cassette players, recorders, records—are all highly profitable foundations for a business, within the rules I've prescribed. You can begin at home, or as part of somebody else's store, or in your own store. Wherever it is, it is easy to expand from whatever kind of merchandise you choose to begin with. Starting with health and beauty aids and cosmetics leads easily to Timex watches, with counter-top fixtures supplied by the manufacturer. Then on to pantyhose, men's socks, calculators and chemicals.

I want to emphasize again that this huge classification of chemicals is, in my opinion, much underestimated by most retailers. If you do carry them, you should try to carry *all* of them in the famous brands. When I say "all," I would even include housewares as well as automotive chemicals. I think they complement each other. For example, let's assume you have begun a housewares store, and that you also carry all the cleaning agents used at home—deodorants, polishes for furniture and woodwork, and most importantly, sink and washing machine detergents. To these add the chemicals used for automobile care (waxes, motor lubricants and similar items) because these things sell every day of the week and represent a remarkable turnover, creating traffic for the store.

At the risk of repeating myself, there are some other important recommendations I want to make:

> *Never be complacent about cleanliness in your store. Whether it's the front or the back, the interior, the shelves, the merchandise, the windows, be rigid about insisting on cleanliness everywhere on the premises.*

> *Pay maximum attention to your presentation. Display in any case ought not to be a chore; it should be something you enjoy, otherwise you ought to ask yourself whether you're in the right business.*

> *Take time out to visit other local stores and see what they're doing. With knowledge gained from observation, plus your own skills, you should be able to make handsome and attractive presentations which will enhance the character of your store–and give yourself a feeling of pride and accomplishment.*

> *Don't be lazy.*

A Word on Advertising

When you open your store, one of the first problems you'll have to think about is advertising. It is important because I think it goes without saying that you won't be opening on the busiest street in town where most of the people pass by all day long. It's also impractical to believe that at the beginning you will have the resources to spend a great deal of money advertising your store. But there is something that can be done, nonetheless. The merchandise you'll be carrying will be well known and well advertised, and your customers will understand the value they're getting because your prices will be very reasonable and competitive. You can itemize your products and their prices, then make these lists available to firms in the neighborhood.

I did just that when E. J. Korvette was started, giving my lists to all the industrial companies in the area. You should go to office managers, personnel managers and purchasing departments. These three constitute the people who have the responsibility for disseminating such information among the employees. You don't need money to do this; all it requires is determination and energy.

To remind you again, the merchandise we've been talking about is available from distributors. Some of it can be bought directly from the manufacturer at a savings, which will probably not be very large. The distributor is your best ally. Consult the list of distributors at the back of this book, remembering that you will need to supplement it with your local telephone yellow pages. If you speak to any of these people, you'll find them only too happy to tell you about other distributors in the vicinity of your store.

In this chapter, then, are the basic principles you need to go into the retailing business for yourself. Now let's get down to the details.

7

Are You the Type?

As this book testifies, I'm a firm advocate of going into business for yourself, but I know that the simple desire to do so is not enough. Before you commit yourself to a career in retailing you need to study the field and your own strengths and weaknesses very carefully. It may seem to you as I go along that I'm being contradictory, that I'm telling you to stick to something you know, which is the opposite of what I did in creating the E. J. Korvette enterprises. But remember that in the beginning I *did* start with something I knew, using in that first store on Forty-sixth Street the knowledge I had gained in my father's place on Lexington Avenue. As I went into other areas of business I wasn't always successful, as my story relates. Sometimes I had to abandon projects or lines of activity, but I did so in a way that guaranteed I would not be hurt financially. I never had so much invested in any one enterprise that it would cause financial damage should one part of the business fail.

Before you open your doors for business, I particularly recommend that you get the booklets published by the federal government's Small Business Administration (S.B.A.). A list of their field offices is at the end of this chapter; addresses and telephone numbers are in local telephone directories under "United States Government," or you can write to the Small Business Administration, Washington, D.C., 20416. The S.B.A. also helps the small businessman get bank credit and capital, conducts workshops and provides information about new management approaches through counseling, courses and publications.

Some Qualifications

I believe people who are thinking of a retailing career ought to approach it with a proper degree of humility. They should understand that a good merchandiser will always be a beginner because the more he knows about his business, the more he realizes how little he knows. The world doesn't stand still long enough for any businessman to stop being a beginner. Products change, packaging materials and methods change, merchandising techniques change, markets change, and so do people. It's constantly necessary in a business to "begin again," with one aspect of it or another. Because of the need to be a perpetual learner, it's important for a prospective retailer to master as much information as possible about the business before he takes the final step and becomes an owner.

My aim here is to help you decide whether you really want to take on the responsibilities and risks that go with owning a business, and to give you a head start toward rounding out your knowledge of the problems involved in starting and owning a business.

First, let me say, there's the good news to consider. To run a business of your own brings a sense of independence, an opportunity to make free use of your own ideas. You'll be the boss; you can't be fired. Furthermore, you'll have an opportunity to earn a higher income because you can collect a salary plus a profit or return on your investment. There is, too, the great satisfaction of building a valuable investment for which there will be a market.

As a boss, you'll be able to adopt new ideas quickly. Since your enterprise will almost certainly be a small business, at least in the beginning, you won't have a large, unwieldy organization to re-train every time you want to try something new. If an idea doesn't work, you can drop it quickly. That kind of flexibility will be one of your greatest assets.

Those are some of the advantages and pleasures of operating your own business. But now for the bad news. If you have employees, you'll have to meet a payroll week after week. You must always, in addition, have enough money to pay creditors—the person who sells you goods or materials; the dealer who furnishes fixtures and equipment for your store; the landlord, if you rent, or the mortgage holder, if you've bought your place of business; the publisher who runs your advertisements; the tax collector; and so on. Sometimes the list seems endless.

You will have to accept sole responsibility for all the final decisions. Wrong judgments on your part can result in losses not only to yourself, but possibly to your employees, creditors, and customers as well. Moreover, you alone must withstand any adverse situations caused by circumstances beyond your control, factors such as depressed economic conditions or strong competition in your field.

To overcome these disadvantages and keep your business profitable means long hours of hard work. It's a truism that when you become your own boss you'll be working longer hours than you did when you worked for someone else. Matters may improve later on, but don't count on it.

From my own experience, I can tell you that the most important thing I did to keep my independence and pay the bills was to turn over the merchandise just as rapidly as possible. During the first five years, the inventories were turned over slightly less than 30 times, consequently we had large sums of available money in the bank. This gave us considerable leverage with vendors because we could pay them in cash. Vendors who were in need of money often came to us and offered special discounts to get that cash payment. It is sound advice to predicate all your planning on rapid turnover of merchandise.

Considering all of these factors, good and bad, the first question you need to answer before you start to establish your own business and become a retailer is, quite simply, "Am I the type?" As the prospective firm's most important employee, it's crucial that you rate yourself more critically than any other prospective worker. You will have to appraise your own strong and weak points. If you recognize that you're weak in salesmanship, for example, you should know it and cover the deficiency by hiring the best sales talent you can afford.

A study of small business managers and owners has shown that the successful ones have certain personality characteristics in superior quantities. Five qualities show a significant correlation with success:

DRIVE—is a quality composed of responsibility, vigor, initiative, persistence and health.

THINKING ABILITY—consists of original, creative, critical and analytical thinking.

HUMAN RELATIONS ABILITY—encompasses emotional stability, sociability, cautiousness, personal relations, consideration, cheerfulness, cooperation and tact.

COMMUNICATIONS ABILITY—is composed of verbal comprehension, oral communication and written communication.

TECHNICAL KNOWLEDGE—is the information a manager

possess about the physical process of producing goods or services, and his ability to use this information purposefully.

All these capacities can be developed, so that your chances for success will be increased. Drive, for example, has long been considered important to effective performance, but its development, which really means increasing your achievement motivation, depends on setting the right kind of goals for yourself.

The individually owned retail store is essentially a one-man show, consequently your success will depend almost entirely on your own efforts. You'll have to be a specialist in several aspects of your business, and reasonably expert in all the other areas. Even with those qualifications, not everyone has that certain quality that makes him click as his own boss. And if you don't have what it takes as a store owner, it's certainly better to discover this before you tie up your life's savings, or a bank's money, in a failure.

Salesmanship

Probably the basic talent, and the most important attribute, required to operate your own store is salesmanship. Ask yourself honestly now:

Are you a good salesman?

Can you project your sincerity to your customer, so that he feels confident about buying from you?

Will he feel that you're making an honest recommendation, and not trying to sell him something you want to get rid of—the result of a buying mistake you've made—or pushing a product designed to make money for the store without giving full value to the purchaser?

Do you believe that customers are one of the most valuable assets a store can have and should be treated as such?

Do you have an air of friendly confidence that will make people glad to buy from you and happy to return to your store for future purchases?

A good salesman slants his sales approach to the product feature or benefit that will have the greatest appeal to each customer. You should be able to sense what price range and kind of merchandise the customer will find most acceptable and present it in a way that will forestall or overcome resistance. You should have the ability to communicate your ideas in a clear and interesting way, so that the customer's interest in your sales and service will be aroused.

My own success as a salesman can be accounted for simply by the fact that I'm very good at it; fortunately, I had other excellent salesmen to help me. But there's a way to measure how good you have to be. When we first started E. J. Korvette, I calculated that, if we averaged a dollar in profit on every sale regardless of how large or small the individual sales might be, we would be doing well if we made 100 sales a day. Consequently, our overall concentration was on making sales to meet that quota, and surpass it as much as possible.

What we did with washing machines was a good example. We sold them at a $3 profit, and all we looked for was that $3. They came in carload lots of 60, and we sold at least a carload every week. Similarly, our vacuum cleaners were bought in carload lots at a price which enabled us to sell them at a figure less than the customer would have had to pay if he bought them wholesale. There were even some retailers who came to us and bought a few because it was cheaper for them, even with their markup added. Naturally, we were not eager to do such favors for competitors, and these retailers had to send emissaries disguised as ordinary retail customers.

New Roles

Another important function you'll have to carry out as a retailer is buying the product you're going to sell. You'll have to know what people will buy, how much they'll be willing to spend, and how they will learn about what you have to offer. You must have the accompanying ability to use money well, to conserve your resources and spend them wisely. For that, you'll need the ability to sense future trends with some accuracy. It will be necessary to know what will sell, which brands you should carry, in what quantities, and at what particular time.

You will have to develop the knack, if you don't already have it, of presenting your stock in such a way that it seems better than your competitors', or at least different. Some retailers accomplish this through pricing, some with displays, some by means of combined offers. If you're a successful promoter, suppliers will make you all kinds of offers that will add to your profits. Business is where you find it. In whatever organizations you join, you can let people know that you're in business. Remember that everyone is a consumer. If you're a good mixer, you may get customers who wouldn't otherwise come to your store.

You may or may not know how to display your wares in the store and in your windows so that a customer will feel that he *must* buy before he leaves the store. If you don't, you can get help from your suppliers, or from a professional display man. The important thing is to recognize the importance of display and of planning far enough ahead so that you can coordinate your displays with seasonal and holiday merchandising opportunities.

A similar situation may exist with advertising. Quite possibly you won't be able to prepare the ads yourself because you lack the training, time or both. But you should have a good idea of what makes a selling ad, and you can get help in preparing one from an advertising agency or the newspaper in which you advertise. The important thing is to know what effect you want to achieve.

For example, when we first opened our store on Forty-sixth Street, I got out a large mailing to all the purchasing agents in our area, hoping they would convey to their company's employees the values we were making available to them. We also sent listings of those values to personnel managers and office managers, asking if they would post them on office bulletin boards. From that beginning, we relied on word of mouth to produce customers, and as I've described, they were soon clogging the aisles and standing on the stairs. If you can generate that kind of word-of-mouth buying, the battle is more than half over. I never used conventional advertising until after I had been in business for five years.

Successful retailers are sticklers for detail. You'll have to concentrate on the most exacting procedures in the midst of a store's customary hustle and bustle. Dusting, for example, is one of the most disagreeable chores, but it's important. It's endless, too. As soon as you finish, you have to start all over again. The premises must be scrupulously clean and well arranged all the time. You'll never be able to skip your own daily shave, and you will have to insist that your staff maintain a personal appearance that radiates cleanliness and confidence. Make up your mind that there will always be something to do—dozens of big and little jobs, and as many interruptions. You should be a person who doesn't get easily sidetracked and forget where he left off, and certainly not one of those people who starts many jobs and finishes few. You need to keep all those jobs in the back of your mind so you can slip them in whenever you have a few minutes.

To be successful, you have to get to your store early so that you'll get a good start before the day's routine begins, and you'll have to stay after hours more often than not, and take work home if necessary. Obviously, you must be someone not easily discouraged, who thrives on stress and competition. This takes plenty of inner drive and determination.

A good manager of a business understands operating expenses and their control. You may be working in a business where profits are determined in pennies and nickels, not dollars. It's extremely important to be able to plan and coordinate all the activities of a store so that an efficient, smooth-running operation can be maintained. The good manager also knows how to win the cooperation of other people—customers, employees, suppliers, all the people with whom he has dealings of one kind or another. He makes decisions without difficulty and accepts the responsibility for their outcome. He handles his finances so that he has the money he needs at the time he needs it. It takes even temperament to accomplish these things. You will have to be able to control your temper and your tongue when you're dealing with unreasonable people.

Here's a further handy check list that will help you to survey yourself as a potential retailer. Be honest, now:

Are you a self-starter?

How do you feel about other people?

Can you lead others?

Can you take responsibility?

How good an organizer are you?

How good a worker are you?

Can you make decisions?

Can people trust what you say?

Can you stick with it?

How good is your health?

My advice is not to take this list as a set of rigid requirements—you might give up before you start. Nobody is going to score 100 percent on every item in this set of standards. If you're an intelligent person and devote yourself to the business you're starting, all of these characteristics, to whatever degree you possess them, will come together. Nevertheless, a good way to check yourself in advance is to imagine that you are sitting down with a complete stranger to whom you've turned for advice about going into business. No doubt he will be asking these questions and probably others—questions you should be asking yourself. Examine the answers you're giving now in the light of that situation. After rating yourself a second time, ask a friend to have you rated by several people who know you well, and who are capable of evaluating you objectively. They should be guaranteed anonymity. The results may startle you, but they will be a valuable check on your perceptions of yourself.

If you keep in mind that it's your money and your career that are on the line, you'll be able to avoid wishful thinking in these evaluations. Accept your weak points, and prepare to compensate for them by planning to hire people whose strong points will offset your weak ones. But if you're weak in too many of the attributes needed to manage a business, it's far better to accept that fact and not undertake the venture at all than to plunge ahead and lose your money.

Choosing Your Business

But let's suppose that you've passed the personal inventory test and concluded that you have the qualities necessary to become a successful retailer. The next question is, what business should you choose? You might begin by writing out a summary of your background and experience, including everything obtained from jobs, school and even your hobbies. Then write down what you'd like to do. Try to match up what you'd like to do with what you've done. If you choose a business you don't really like, your lack of enthusiasm for it can well lead to failure. Remember that the more experience and training you've had which can be put to direct use in operating a particular enterprise, the better your chances of success will be. That, of course, was why I started out in luggage and leather goods—the only business I knew anything about.

The best way to obtain knowledge of a business is through actual experience in it. If you feel otherwise qualified but don't have enough training, try to find a job working for someone else in the business you're considering, preferably in a well-managed, successful company. Then absorb as much management know-how as you possibly can.

Education helps, too. While there are no educational requirements for starting your own business, it's generally recognized that the more education you've had, the better equipped you will be. For example, in most businesses you must know how to figure interest and discounts, keep simple but adequate records, and conduct necessary correspondence. Knowledge of these and other helpful subjects are most often acquired through formal education, whether at night school, in adult education, by correspondence or on-the-job experience.

I know that not having a formal education beyond high school hurt me. As the years went by, the knowledge I might have gained from a college business administration curriculum, or for that matter from department store experience, would have enabled me to plan and organize better. Looking back I can see that many of the mistakes I made would not have occurred if I had the proper education, and even though I was able to start a small but successful business on what I had learned from my father, I still think the value of formal education can't be underestimated.

Finally, begin with what you're prepared or equipped to offer. Ask yourself what you can do with your present preparation. Seek an objective answer to the question of whether anyone wants the services you are able to render, and find out whether these services can be adapted to present trends in the market.

You should make an earnest effort to determine, as nearly as you can, whether customers will like the kind of business or service you want to establish. It should be a business in tune with the times, and a field in which expansion can be logically expected. Study whatever surveys have been made, and seek as much advice and counsel as you can get from qualified people.

Again, let me advise you to use the tremendous resources of the Small Business Administration. A list of the cities in which their field offices are located follows:

SMALL BUSINESS ADMINISTRATION FIELD OFFICES

Agana, Guam	Fairbanks, Alaska	Nashville, Tenn.
Albuquerque, N. Mex.	Fargo, N. Dak.	Newark, N.J.
Anchorage, Alaska	Gulfport, Miss.	New Orleans, La.
Atlanta, Ga.	Harlingen, Tex.	New York, N.Y.
Augusta, Maine	Harrisburg, Pa.	Oklahoma City, Okla.
Baltimore, Md.	Hartford, Conn.	Omaha, Nebr.
Birmingham, Ala.	Hato Rey, P.R.	Philadelphia, Pa.
Boise, Idaho	Helena, Mont.	Phoenix, Ariz.
Boston, Mass.	Honolulu, Hawaii	Pittsburgh, Pa.
Buffalo, N.Y.	Houston, Tex.	Portland, Oreg.
Casper, Wyo.	Indianapolis, Ind.	Providence, R.I.
Charleston, W. Va.	Jackson, Miss.	Rapid City, S. Dak.
Charlotte, N.C.	Jacksonville, Fla.	Richmond, Va.
Chicago, Ill.	Kansas City, Mo.	St. Louis, Mo.
Cincinnati, Ohio	Knoxville, Tenn.	Salt Lake City, Utah
Clarksburg, W. Va.	Las Vegas, Nev.	San Antonio, Tex.
Cleveland, Ohio	Little Rock, Ark.	San Diego, Calif.
Columbia, S.C.	Los Angeles, Calif.	San Francisco, Calif.
Columbus, Ohio	Louisville, Ky.	Seattle, Wash.
Concord, N.H.	Lubbock, Tex.	Sioux Falls, S. Dak.
Corpus Christi, Tex.	Madison, Wis.	Spokane, Wash.
Dallas, Tex.	Marquette, Mich.	Springfield, Ill.
Denver, Colo.	Marshall, Tex.	Syracuse, N.Y.
Des Moines, Iowa	Miami, Fla.	Washington, D.C.
Detroit, Mich.	Milwaukee, Wis.	Wichita, Kans.
Elmira, N.Y.	Minneapolis, Minn.	Wilkes-Barre, Pa.
El Paso, Tex.	Montpelier, Vt.	Wilmington, Del.

For address and telephone numbers of the field offices, look under "United States Government" in the appropriate telephone directories.

8

Getting Started

YOU'VE DECIDED THAT YOU'RE THE KIND OF PERSON who can operate a business on your own, you've assessed your overall chances for success and you've chosen the kind of business you want to establish. It's time, then, to turn to some of the practical problems involved in starting out. You'll have to determine how much money you'll need to launch yourself and find out where you can obtain it. You will also have to settle on what form of business organization you will be setting up, and then, of course, answer the important question of where you are going to locate. In later chapters, I will go into the details of some of these problems, but let's survey them all right now.

Estimating Your Costs

First, how much money will you need? The answer to this question deserves your most careful study and investigation. It's hard to specify an average amount because circumstances may differ from business to business. Money needs, for example, vary according to the kind of merchandise or services offered, the income level of your customers, your own connections with the trade, the location of the business, general economic conditions at the time you intend to start and many other factors.

Generally, a new business grows slowly at the start. If you overestimate sales, you're likely to invest too much in initial inventory and commit yourself to heavier operating expenses then your actual sales volume justifies.

Some people draw a regular monthly salary and take out the rest of their net profits either at irregular intervals or regularly at the end of every year. Still others reinvest a part of net profits in the business. In any case, you should make a regular allowance for your salary and enter it as the first item of expense. Other salaries and wages should be entered as the second item. Family members who may be assisting you should be paid at the prevailing wage rate, or else the value of their services should be added to your drawings as proprietor.

Besides putting down your continuing monthly expenses, in figuring how much you'll need to start you will also have to add in your non-recurring expenses, that is, those which are going to occur only once. Fixtures and equipment are examples. You can get advice about layout and the selection of fixtures and equipment from representatives of equipment manufacturers and trade associations. In the same way, when you estimate your initial inventory, you can get valuable suggestions from prospective suppliers.

When it's all added up, your available money should exceed the estimated cash needed to start by a safe margin—"safe" depending somewhat on how conservative you are, how much risk you want to take. Remember that in addition to your initial investment you'll need enough in reserve to carry the business until it's self-supporting. Do not underestimate the amount of cash you will need. Remember that it's going to be necessary to hire enough employees to keep your business in operation, to invest in proper equipment, to maintain an adequate stock of merchandise or materials so that you can build sales volume, to take advantage of any discounts offered by creditors, and to grant credit to customers so that you can meet competition.

Finding a Location

Now that you've decided what kind of business you're going into and how much it will cost you, the next step is to find a location. You may have already decided that you want to start in your home town, or in some part of the country where you think you'd prefer to live. Fine, but be sure the community you have selected needs the business you plan to open.

Picking a location involves, first, selecting the town or city, then choosing an area within it and finally selecting a site in that area. Let's begin with the town itself.

It would be nice if you had the money to obtain the detailed and sophisticated scientific studies that large companies employ, but small operators have to evaluate locations as best they can. It's possible to get informed help, however. Wholesalers and manufacturers who supply merchandise and equipment are a prime source of this kind of information. So are federal, state and local governments. All these will point you toward other sources.

An important first consideration is population. You should find out how fast the town or city in which you plan to locate is growing, whether it's growing at all or worse, declining. You need to know, too, the composition of that population by age, occupation and income. These factors will have an effect on your sales volume. But you'll have to remember, too, that if your business is going to be regional or beyond the town you're locating in, the local statistics will have to be supplemented with others. Still, there are some facts that will be applicable, such as the condition of the local labor market, the wage scales and the town's accessibility to freight carriers.

The Bureau of Census figures are a help. They'll tell you how many directly competitive businesses there already are in your proposed location. They will also give you such important data as the relationship between the town's population and the number of businesses in it. If there's a grocery for every 1,500 inhabitants, for example, a new store would not be as attractive a proposition as an optical goods store, if the present ratio for this kind of enterprise is 1 to every 60,000 inhabitants. But remember these Census Bureau figures are countrywide averages and may not necessarily be true in a particular town. They simply show how the number of inhabitants per store varies in different kinds of businesses.

You'll also want to look into the matter of environmental factors, that is, whether the local utilities are adequate for your purposes, whether there are enough parking facilities near your location, how good the police and fire protection are, and such other factors as schools, cultural and community activities. I offer this as a kind of general checklist. Obviously, if a man opens a grocery store, one thing he can be sure of is that the environmental statistics he begins with are going to alter as time goes on because neighborhoods change and consumer demands shift. Think of these factors, then, and try to assess them intelligently, but don't let them worry you excessively at the beginning.

More specifically, however, local taxes and average rents are going to be figured in your preliminary cost estimates, and you'll want to know about such things as zoning regulations, the general business climate in the town, and whether it appears to be a lively, growing community or a depressed one. Chambers of commerce, state development agencies and similar organizations will give you information that will help to answer all these questions, but remember the source and take what you hear and read with a grain of salt so you can test it against less self-interested sources.

Once you've picked your town and satisfied yourself that it's the place for you and your business to be, you'll need to find the particular location in it that will best suit your needs. If it's a small town, there's likely to be only one retail area and consequently not much choice. If it's a city of any size, there will be outlying shopping centers to consider as well as the downtown area, and possible locations on neighborhood streets or main highways.

If you're going to locate in a shopping center, remember that it is pre-planned as a merchandising unit, and some of your problems such as on-site parking will already be solved. In some cases, there is also weather protection. These and other advantages provided by the developer are offset, however, by limitations on your freedom. Rather than owning your own store, typically, you'll be a tenant in a development and will have to pay your share of its budget. You'll also have to follow a set of rules governing store hours, window lighting and the placement of signs.

There may be difficulty in getting a place in a shopping center at all. The developers and owners choose successful retailers, and you'll have to convince them you're going to be, if you don't have a previous track record. If they think you don't qualify financially, it may be necessary to get the help of the Small Business Administration's lease guarantee program. The nearest S.B.A. office will tell you about it.

In choosing the kind of shopping area you want for your business, the location will be at least partly determined by the kind of merchandise you're selling. Obviously, clothing, jewelry and department stores are going to be more successful in central shopping districts, while grocery and drug stores, filling stations and bakeries do better on main and neighborhood streets away from these districts. Furniture, grocery and hardware stores usually pay low rent per square foot, but cigar and drug stores, women's furnishings and department stores pay high rent. In the town you've chosen, look over the successful stores selling your kind of merchandise, and you'll get a better idea of where you should be.

Location is also determined by the size of the store. If your original investment is very small, it may be impossible to get enough sales volume to justify high business center rents, so you would then have to go farther out, if it's a large city. Otherwise, switch to a smaller community, where rentals would be more in line with the size of the investment.

Once you've decided on the area, get as much information about it as you can, particularly as to the existing competition and their present sales volumes. You'll want to know, too, how many blocks in the area you can expect to draw customers from, and just how many people there are in the area, whether it's a stabilized or growing neighborhood, and the mix of the people in it, especially what they do for a living, and their ages. These facts will give you some idea of their buying power, but it will also help to know what the average rent is for homes in the area, the average real estate taxes, the number of automobiles and, if you can get the figures, the per capita income. Finally, it will be necessary to know about the area's zoning ordinances, its parking problems, its transportation facilities, and any physical barriers like hills or bridges that may affect business.

As I've said, the usual sources for all this information are chambers of commerce, trade associations, real estate companies, local newspapers, banks and city officials, but always bearing in mind that whatever they tell you may well be colored by self-interest. Sharp personal observation is a big help. It would be especially helpful if the Census Bureau has developed census tract information for your particular area. These tracts are small, permanently established geographical areas in large cities and their environs, for which the Bureau provides population and housing characteristics.

So now you have the community and the area pinned down. Next comes the actual site. The task is to find something that is both suitable and available. You may not have too much choice, but the possibilities have to be carefully assessed. Many of the criteria are the same ones you've already applied to the area—that is, nearness of competition, flow of traffic, parking facilities, location on the street and the transportation situation. Others relate directly to the building itself— its physical aspects, the kind of lease offered and how much it will cost you and whatever you can find out about the building's past history. If it's been vacant for a long time, you'll want to know why. If it's been occupied by different kinds of stores for short periods, find out why there was such a rapid changeover. Obviously, no one should try to do business on a site that's a proven loser. Nor do you want vacant buildings next door or too close to your place of business. They're bad neighbors.

Preparing Your Store for Business

Once you've signed the lease, the first concerns are the layout of the store and the fixtures needed. I've already discussed these in relation to the E. J. Korvette stores, but a little more detail is required here. You should know that the person who sells you the fixtures will provide an architect's services in measuring your shop. He will ask which departments you want and how much space should be alloted to each. He will then give you a rough floor plan, with wall cabinets and showcases designed to fit. Lighting fixtures have to be planned for the best possible display purposes. Colors must be chosen for the interior, with the store front and display windows designed to harmonize with the inside. You may want to hire an independent architect to help you, if you don't feel confident about such matters. He'll help you design the store, get estimates from the fixture manufacturers, and supervise the installation. An alternative is to deal with a manufacturer of store interiors; he usually has a designer who will help you plan the layout.

Whoever you get to do the job, don't forget that the selling area has to be as large as possible, with sufficient space reserved for stockroom and offices. The stockroom space should be large enough that you can borrow from it later on if you need more selling space. In any case, you'll have to estimate the number of customers you can expect to have in the store at any one time, and provide enough space for your sales staff to cope with the traffic.

Theft

As every retailer knows, an important problem often overlooked by beginners is the high percentage of shoplifting. A New York department store deployed a large task force of observers to follow customers from the time they entered the store until they left, and discovered that one out of every eight stole something. Pilferage is such a serious problem in most stores that as many precautions as possible must be taken to minimize the risk. It's impossible to eliminate it. Self-service items are particularly vulnerable, but you'll have to weigh the losses against the sales that would not be made if the merchandise wasn't in plain sight, and the selling time and expense involved in selling it the usual way.

Many stores use convex mirrors to discourage shoplifting. Not many thieves are caught that way, but the presence of the mirrors discourages many from trying. Larger stores in big cities use security guards. Guards, even if no more than a night watchman, are certainly necessary in many places for nights, weekends and holidays. If a store is too small for even that minimal expense, then get the best available locks for transoms, doors and windows. If you're in doubt ask the police what to get; they're specialists. If your salespeople and supervisors in the store are constantly alert, that will be the best protection you can hope for, in the long run. Security also depends on the size of the store.

In our first five years, before we began to expand, we had little protection aside from our own vigilance. It was a different matter when we were running big, impersonal department store operations. Then it became necessary to use every protective device that was available and applicable to our situation.

In the case of merchandise in windows, obviously it's impractical to take everything out and put it back in again every day. Many stores use metal screens or folding gates for protection. Gates shut off the view, but with metal screens window shoppers can see what you have on display. The mesh needs to be fine enough, however, so thieves can't get through it to break the window.

Other retailers connect their shops with a central alarm agency, so that sensing devices set off an alarm in the agency office whenever someone tries to break in and guards are sent within minutes. Exactly what kind of protection you need depends, of course, on the kind of neighborhood your store is in, and the crime rate in that area. But in any case, you'll feel more secure and your insurance premiums will be lower if you provide yourself with the best protection available.

Insurance and Legal Problems

One thing new retailers discover, if they're too inexperienced to know about it beforehand, is that having your own business isn't all buying and selling. A lot of it is drudge work in the office, involving all kinds of documents, and the smaller the operation, the more of it you'll have to do.

The whole complicated business of insurance is one of these problems. A good insurance broker can help you plan your program, but the planning will take hours of your time. The law requires you to have some kinds of insurance. The important thing here is to have a broker you can trust, and then work out an overall program with him.

Far more burdensome, however, is dealing with government regulations, whether federal, state, local or all three. Since regulations vary widely from one place to another, you'll have to know which ones affect you. This means using the services of a lawyer who will see to it that your business complies with whatever regulations affect it—more time and money. The lawyer will help you with your contracts with the fixture man, the air-conditioning engineer and the others who do contract work for you. So many problems that require legal advice come up in business that I can only urge you to get a good lawyer you like and trust at the start, so that you'll be getting your advice from someone who is completely familiar with you and your enterprise.

Store Hours

Another problem you'll have to solve before you open for business is the question of store hours. That will depend, of course, on the working and shopping patterns of your potential customers, and the hours should be geared to them. If they're primarily office workers, for example, the store ought to be open about a half hour before their day begins. If they're mostly housewives, however, you won't need to open before 9:30 or even 10 a.m., since many have morning work to do before they can get to the stores. Most stores do what their neighbors do in matters like keeping shops open on one weekday evening, or possibly on Sunday, where local or state Blue Laws don't prohibit it (providing they're enforced). Patterns vary. Saturday is the big shopping day in some locations, while in downtown office districts there is no business on Saturday. Shopping centers often stay open until 9 p.m. to accommodate people who can't get to them during the working day. These stores, and those on highways, are often open weekends and holidays during the day and part of the evening.

It isn't necessary for you to follow any of these patterns simply for the sake of conforming. In your particular business, it may be unprofitable for you to follow the hours your neighbors keep. You should be open only during those hours when there's enough business to justify it. That means some compromise, however, between profitability and your customers' shopping habits. It's sometimes a delicate judgment you'll have to make.

Buying a Store

The obvious alternative to starting your own business is to buy one that's already in operation. All the factors already discussed apply equally should you make that decision, but there are other factors to be considered as well.

There is good news and bad news about buying a going business. Here's the good news. You may get a bargain if the owner is really anxious to sell. Certainly time and effort will be saved on your part. Customers already exist so you won't have to wait for them to discover your shop, as you would with a new business. The seller may be able to give you valuable information based on his own experience—but remember that it's likely to be much more reliable after the sale of the business is made.

There may be bad news too. Misrepresentation by the owner and your own mistakes in appraising the business may cost you money. An owner and his store may have a bad reputation that will be difficult to overcome. The location itself may not be a good one, but I've already given you a check list to guard against that disadvantage. Fixtures and equipment may be in bad condition or may have to be changed for some other reason, and that adds to the initial cost. The merchandise already in the store may be poorly selected and will have to be replaced.

If the good outweighs the bad and you decide to go ahead, the question is, how much should you pay for a going business? Its profit potential is the first consideration. Equipment and inventory are important as they affect future profits, but the seller may well be asking something for good will, an intangible asset, and that, too, has to be estimated in terms of those future profits. There is also the problem of any liabilities you may have to take over.

In looking toward the future, and trying to determine potential, the object is to try to estimate as nearly as possible what sales and profits you can expect over the next few years. How do you estimate future profits? It's a chancy business, at best, but you begin by analyzing the balance sheets and profit-and-loss statements of the owner for at least the previous five years; 10 years is even better. Not all owners keep accurate records, by any means, so you may be compelled to get copies of their income tax returns. You need to know the rate of return on investment, and how it compares with the rate you might expect to get for your money if it were invested in something else, as well as how it compares with averages for other businesses of a similar kind.

You will want to know whether the store's sales have been increasing or decreasing, and whether it's getting a proper share of the area's business. Again, you'll have to use your information about competition, population and the purchasing power of the customers in the area, plus some kind of informed estimate of the outlook for increased sales.

Profits, of course, have to be looked into. Are they too low, and if so, what are the prospects of increasing them? You'll want to know whether the profits, whatever they are, have been reasonably consistent over a period of time. Sudden rises or falls will have to be explained. If they have been consistent but are now leveling off or decreasing, you'll want to know why.

Expense ratios are another good index. Compare each expense classification with the average for the trade. If there are discrepancies, talk about them with the seller. That may well bring to light operating problems you will want to know about. But don't be discouraged completely if the store's past profit records aren't favorable. The reason may be bad management, which you will expect to improve. On the other hand, if the profits have been high and consistent, run up your caution flag and ask yourself why the owner is selling in that case. In any event, don't let that fact impel you to pay more for the business than it's really worth.

The seller should give you a projected profit-and-loss statement for the next 12 months. In doing this, he'll be using data probably not available to you, but you'll have to compare it with your own estimate, remembering that his figuring of profits is practically certain to be more optimistic than yours. With this information, however, it will be possible to compute working capital requirements for every month. Estimate the value of your assets and liabilities at the end of this period, and figure the estimated return on your investment. If you think you're going to need more money immediately to make the business profitable, add that amount to the price. In the end, you'll have a fairly reliable estimate of future profits on which you can base your offer.

I'm sure that not everyone who starts out in retailing has the kind of expertise to make the judgments I've been describing here. If not, you'll need the services of an experienced accountant who knows what to look for in the books and how to project future business.

If you buy, what do you get for your money? In terms of tangible assets, there will be merchandise inventory, equipment and fixtures, and supplies. When credit is involved, you'll also take over accounts receivable. You should be sure, consequently, about the condition of the inventory you're acquiring, whether the stock is timely, fresh and well balanced, whether you'll have to dispose of some of it at a loss. Appraise it carefully, price every item separately, and put a reasonable value on it. The inventory ought to be what the trade calls "aged"— that is, divided according to the amount of time each group of items has been in stock, from less than 6 months to more than 18 months. It's axiomatic in retailing that the older the inventory, the less its value.

Be sure to examine equipment and fixtures carefully. They're second-hand goods, remember, and worth only a percentage of their original value. Check them to see if they work. You'll want to know how much they have depreciated, and whether they are actually obsolete. Office equipment, for example, may be in working condition but so obsolete that it is inefficient; replacement parts, if needed, may be hard to find. Store fixtures go out of date rapidly, and you need new ones to get customers. Allow for depreciation and obsolescence, then set a fair valuation on all the fixtures and equipment. It may be that since so much money will be tied up in them the business won't justify the investment. Be absolutely sure to find out if there are any mortgages on fixtures and equipment.

As for assets like accounts receivable, credit records, sales records, mailing lists or leases, the best advice is to investigate them thoroughly. You'll want to know, for example, how many of the accounts receivable are so old that they'll be impossible to collect.

Then, finally, we come to that most intangible factor, "good will," or what the owner believes the public thinks about his business. Don't confuse it with "net worth," which is the difference between dollar values of assets and liabilities. It's true enough that good will is a valuable asset, but you'll have to decide how much you want to pay for it. I don't know of any method to measure it, but certainly you should try to check on whether it's as good as the owner claims it is. Ask customers, if you can, and bankers who deal with the business, and anyone else you think might give you an informed, unprejudiced opinion. Most important, perhaps, is the question of how much "good will" remains after the business changes hands. If it was generated through the owner's personality, you'll have to take that into account. If it is attached to the business itself, that's another story.

One practical test can be applied. Compare the price the owner is asking with the business's past profits, then figure out how long it will be before "good will" can be paid for out of profits, and remember that during that time you'll be working for the former owner, in effect, rather than yourself. You might also judge "good will" by asking yourself how much more income you're likely to get from buying a going business rather than starting a new one.

Be sure to pin down the owner's liabilities and see that his accumulated debts are paid off before you write your check unless you're willing to assume what he owes. These debts could include mortgages, back taxes, liens on the assets and the claims of creditors—as well as any undelivered purchases. You may have to assume a few liabilities in some cases, but if so, the amount should be subtracted from the value of the assets to arrive at the net value.

Net value, however, doesn't mean final price. Reaching that figure means only that you've determined what the business is worth. The other factors affecting the final price can only be determined by means of negotiation.

We are also dealing here with some very personal aspects of the seller and his business. If he had a bad reputation among his employees and suppliers, it may take considerable effort on your part to erase it. It is absolutely essential to have suppliers who will deal with you, and if a franchise is involved, you'll have to obtain assurance that it won't be withdrawn.

Common sense will bring you back to the main question: Why does the owner want to sell? The reason he gives may not be the real one, and only a thorough investigation will disclose the reality. He may say his health is poor and he must have a change of climate, but the facts may be that the neighborhood is changing, or some new civic development or zoning law is going to affect him adversely. Probably you'll never get the whole truth from him. It's better to ask other people you can rely on. Some sellers, it must be added, have sold and then started a new business in competition nearby, and so it's a good idea that the contract should specifically forbid anything like that for a certain period of time in a specified area.

Obviously, a lawyer will be drawing up the final agreement and he will see that all the essential points are covered. However, before you sign it, read it and satisfy yourself that they *are* covered. Here, according to the Small Business Administration, is what such a contract should include:

> A description of what is being sold.
>
> The purchase price.
>
> The method of payment.
>
> A statement of how adjustments are to be handled at the time of closing (adjustments for inventory sold, rent, payroll and insurance premiums).
>
> Buyer's assumption of contracts and liabilities.
>
> Seller's warranties (for example, warranty protection for the buyer against false statements of the seller, inaccurate financial data and undisclosed liabilities).
>
> Seller's obligation and assumption of risk pending closing.
>
> Covenant of seller not to compete.
>
> Time, place and procedure of closing.

You'll have some protection because of the bulk sales law of the state in which you're buying. That prevents the seller from putting the money in his pocket and leaving without paying his creditors. Sellers have to provide a sworn list of creditors. Buyers, in turn, have to give the creditors notice of the impending sale. If this is not done, creditors could conceivably claim the property you bought.

In any event, take possession as soon as possible after you've signed the contract. Don't give the seller any opportunity to deplete the inventory or otherwise create any problems for you.

You'll need your accountant, your lawyer, or both to advise you on the federal income tax consequences of your purchase. The seller should be getting the same kind of advice, because one of the first things he has to think about is how much tax he'll have to pay on his profit from the sale. You, as the buyer, need to be concerned about the tax basis you'll be acquiring. These considerations usually become part of the sale negotiations, since they affect valuation of the business and inevitably bring buyer and seller into conflict.

Buyers and sellers alike would be well advised to study the IRS Tax Guide for small businesses, as well as to consult an income tax expert who may know more about it than an ordinary lawyer or accountant. The income tax laws are so complicated, especially in transactions of this kind, that they can be better understood by specialists. Before the contract is closed, tax planning is highly advisable.

Starting Money

Finally, the deal is made, or it's certainly going to be made, and the time to produce is at hand. At this point, the newcomer to retailing may realize for the first time that he is risking a lot of money and that he is in a position to put himself into a state of lifelong debt.

I don't know a more difficult question to answer than how much money you need to invest in your business. I had $4,000, you'll remember, and that was that. But ordinarily the amount you'll need is determined by location, the size of the business, the amount of planned inventory, the number of employees, and how much you expect to make. Possibly there will be a gap between what you need and what you have. That means a partner or some other kind of help. In any case, it pays not to underestimate the amount of capital you'll need.

If you're renting a store, you'll want enough money to do whatever is necessary in the way of remodeling for your business. Whatever you buy should be of good enough quality to last a minimum of five years. You may have to make a decision about the exterior, too—whether you need money to make it look more attractive, or whether you can let it go with a fresh coat of paint.

Shop around for second-hand fixtures, if that's necessary. There are some good bargains. Sometimes fixture salesmen, if they're smart and honest, can help you set up without maximum expense. The danger here lies in economizing too much. It's poor judgment to skimp on the appearance of your store. The first impression people are going to get of your business depends on how the place looks. They may never get to see the inside if the outside is shabby. They'll just keep walking.

I must admit that I had to compromise appearance for the sake of price in my first stores, and if you recall my account of them, you will remember I wasn't pleased with this arrangement but I could see no alternative. They were poor in appearance, but they were clean. Obviously, only a minimal investment could be made for decor in those early days; when we expanded into larger stores, however, the fixtures became very important. The situation is different today, I believe. A good appearance is essential for almost any store. It must be bright, cheerful and always clean. As a minimum people expect that much.

Much the same can be said of the merchandise you're going to offer, except that inevitably you'll find yourself compromising between what you'd like to have and what you can afford—the same kind of decision your customers make. Wholesalers can be a big help here. As I said earlier, study what other shops carry, especially those of your size and category; it will guide you toward later additions.

Before you start figuring how much money you're going to need, don't forget that there will be several small but annoying expenses to provide for. For example, you'll have to give the landlord several months' security if you're renting. Utility companies demand deposits. There will be local registration and licensing fees, insurance premiums, legal expenses, supplies like stationery, wrapping materials and equipment for keeping records—the list can be formidable.

Don't forget one very important thing. When all these preliminary expenses have been paid, be sure you have money in the bank to cover the probable gap between what the new business takes in and your initial operational costs and living expenses. Usually a new business takes a little time to catch on, and you'll need money to tide you over. But whatever money you have, you can be certain it won't seem like enough. Everything always costs more than you think; unforeseen expenses crop up; there's always something else you need.

As every businessman knows, undercapitalization has been the doom of uncounted enterprises. That's why it's important to include every possible expense in your estimate of what it takes to start. This is a list that should be gone over meticulously again and again. Many people who go into retailing do so on money they saved, but when they have finished their estimate of start-up costs, they frequently find that the money just isn't enough. Then it becomes necessary to turn elsewhere for cash.

In such circumstances, the natural impulse is to approach family or friends, if that's possible, but close connections of blood or friendship should never be permitted to override two basic considerations. One is to make the loan strictly business, with rates of interest and repayment terms clearly specified. The other is to avoid taking advice from whoever makes the loan, otherwise you lose essential control of the business.

If you go to a bank for the money, standard procedures prevail. You will have to establish your credit reputation, and put up some kind of collateral. The banker will want to know such things as how much of your own money you're going to invest, and he'll want to have almost as much information about the business as you possess. Don't be discouraged if you're turned down. It often happens. Try some other banks, and see if you can't learn something from one turndown so you won't make the same mistake next time.

You have to sell yourself to a banker. Even if you're not taking out a loan, it's a good idea to talk with your banker at least once a year, discussing your plans and whatever difficulties you may be having. That will be helpful when you do have to come in for a loan. If that occurs, write out the complete information he will need to make a decision, answering such questions as what you're going to do with the money, when and how you plan to pay it back, whether the amount asked for provides enough leeway for unexpected developments and what the outlook is for you personally, for your business and for the general field you're in.

The Small Business Administration may be able to help you if the banks won't. Management and financial specialists are available to consult with you. You can get counseling whether you're applying for a loan or not, and without charge. For the complete details of S.B.A.'s assistance, write to Small Business Administration, Washington, D. C., 20416.

If you are fortunate enough to have an excellent credit reputation, and if the suppliers are sold on your ability and integrity, you may be able to get your first orders on extended billing or promissory notes, or in some cases on consignment, with the privilege of returning what you can't sell.

Still another kind of help that will ease the budget is the display materials provided by some manufacturers. Most of them offer seasonal units to dress windows and store interiors. There are even display case units you can use as permanent show cases, without cost, thus reducing your fixture expenses.

Is a Partnership for You?

I've been talking thus far from the standpoint of being the sole proprietor of a business. That's the easiest way to start, and it has the added advantage of few legal problems, as well as avoiding the necessity of sharing control or profits. There *are* disadvantages, however. As sole proprietor, you alone are responsible for all the debts of your business, and you risk not only whatever you've invested but everything else you own. It's also more difficult to borrow if you have only your own assets to offer as collateral.

There are other methods of organization, as everyone knows. Most familiar, I suppose, is the partnership, about which a great deal can be said pro and con. There are those who wouldn't take a partner under any circumstances, and others who attribute their success to partnerships. Certainly partners can provide capital, and the right one can be a help in a great many ways, as I well know. Sharing of work hours can be a blessing, and it's reassuring to know that when you're away, the business is in good hands, with someone who shares your responsibility. Some partners may even be able to teach you certain aspects of the business and consequently save you time and money.

There's always an "on the other hand" in partnerships, and the most common is the problem posed by the effort to mesh two personalities which may be in conflict with each other on important points. It is difficult to be in constant business contact with another person day in and day out; it makes marriage seem easy. The record of broken partnerships must be the longest list in the business world.

Practically, you have to ask yourself what your prospective partner is going to bring into the business. It may be that his ability and experience are valuable supplements to yours. Often solid knowledge, background or money are more valuable assets in a partner than simply the fact that he's an old friend you'd like to have with you in the business. Friendships often don't survive a business relationship. Then, too, businesses sometimes aren't really large enough to justify a partnership and to support two people.

Whatever factors may be involved in a partnership, the most important may be your faith in a partner's business judgment and honesty. Without both, there can only be trouble ahead. Remember, you're personally liable for any debts he contracts or any other obligations he incurs as a partner in the business.

Partnerships are formed by legal agreements, which need to be prepared by a lawyer. In fact, you should consult your lawyer to determine whether sole proprietorship, partnership or incorporation is the best way to organize your particular business. A detailed partnership agreement signed by both parties is not required by law, but you should not proceed without it. This agreement should define, among other things, each partner's duties and responsibilities, and how the partnership is to be ended if one withdraws.

I never had partners in my business. By the time we were ready to open our fourth store, I invited employees and vendors alike to invest in the enterprise as a separate corporation. The total capitalization of that store was initially $250,000, of which I put up $25,000. By popular demand of the other shareholders, I held the only voting stock; they agreed that I should make the final decisions. In 18 months, these people not only got their original investments back but a multiple return on it as well.

Incorporating a business is often done as a means of raising additional capital, and has the added advantage of providing you with limited liability. Every stockholder or owner risks only what he invests, but this advantage will have more value later on than it does in the beginning, when your creditors will probably want you to sign obligations personally. An owner is also able to sell or transfer his stock to someone else whenever he chooses, if he has a buyer, and the corporation's activities will not be affected.

There are a few disadvantages in setting up a corporation. One is the cost of doing it (filing the papers alone costs about $200 in most states). Then there are additional taxes applied to corporations, and closer regulation by governmental agencies. Only detailed consultation with your lawyer and accountant can tell you whether incorporation is better for you than acquiring a partner or assuming sole ownership.

9

Some Special Requirements

MOST OF THE SPECIAL REQUIREMENTS for going into retailing have been touched on in earlier chapters, but because they're so important in starting a new business, I think they are worth discussing in more detail. Please understand that this is only basic information. The subjects of laws and regulations, taxes and insurance are so complicated that few people can be expected to master them. You need to have competent, expert help in each one of these areas. But you also need to acquire some basic knowledge of your own so that you'll know what you're looking for.

Licensing and Regulations

One of the first special requirements you will have to worry about is the regulations governing licensing. These will be primarily state and local, if your business is conducted within a single state. Such regulations principally affect operations like retail food stores, places where liquor is served, barber shops, beauty shops, plumbing firms and taxi companies—in brief, service businesses. If your store is simply handling merchandise, it will probably not need a license, but it will be subject to fire, safety and zoning regulations. Licenses for the most part mean paying annual fees, and can be obtained by writing to state, city or county authorities.

There are other laws and regulations that may affect your business. One is the Consumer Credit Protection Act of 1969, commonly known as the "Truth-in-Lending" act, and applies to any business that extends credit to customers. The law prescribes standard terminology for stating your credit terms, so that consumers will be able to compare them.

Another federal law to protect consumers is the "Truth in Fabrics" law which requires textile fiber products to be labeled and advertised in prescribed ways. As a retailer, you'll be sharing responsibility with both the wholesaler and the manufacturer for making sure that where fiber content is concerned, the goods you sell are properly labeled and advertised. The law applies to you if you're advertising wearing apparel or household fabric products in newspapers with interstate circulations, or if you're selling cloth items that have been shipped in interstate commerce, which includes most of them. You should know that this law applies whether or not you are marketing goods across state lines. Consequently, most retailers come under the obligations of the labeling law.

Other consumer protection laws include the Food, Drug and Cosmetics Act and the Flammable Fabrics Act, both of which you should be familiar with. Environmentalists in recent years have been able to get many laws enacted to reduce pollution. Before you go into business, you should find out whether any of these regulations apply to your operation. Make an inquiry to the proper trade association, if there is one, or inquire at the various branches of government which affect you.

There are laws, both federal and state, designed to prohibit or restrict business practices that discourage competition. The federal laws have to do with interstate commerce, while those on the state level concern business within a state. The federal laws are well known to most people: the Sherman, Clayton and Federal Trade Commission acts. Not so familiar are the innumerable state laws governing contracts, combinations, conspiracies in restraint of trade, price discrimination between purchasers of commodities of the same grade and quality, false advertising, disparagement of competitors and misrepresentation. These statutes are constantly being amended, and are further altered by court decisions. You'll need your lawyer to interpret them along with information that may be forthcoming from chambers of commerce or business associations.

A more troublesome area is the whole field of labor relations, where both federal and state laws deal with the settlement of labor disputes, wages, hours, working conditions, fair employment practices and economic security.

Again, most of us are familiar with the major federal laws: the National Labor Relations Act, the Taft-Hartley Act and the Labor Management Reporting and Disclosure Act. But states also have laws affecting collective bargaining and defining unfair labor practices.

Whether or not your employees are covered by the laws prescribing wages, hours and working conditions can be determined by consulting the nearest office of the Wage and Hour and Public Contracts Division of the U.S. Department of Labor. Minimum wages, maximum hours, overtime pay, equal pay, record keeping and child labor are all covered and regulated by the Fair Labor Standards Act. Other statutes, including the Walsh-Healey Public Contracts Act and the Davis-Bacon Act, govern wages, hours and working conditions where government contractors are involved.

Every retailer also needs to know about the Occupational Safety and Health Act of 1970. This federal law provides that employers must provide their employees with a working environment free from recognized hazards that may cause death or serious physical harm, as well as comply with safety and health standards set up by the Act. You can get specific information from the nearest office of the Occupational Safety and Health Administration.

Enough publicity has resulted from the application, or non-application, of the Federal Civil Rights Act of 1964 to make most people, including potential retailers, familiar with it. It is the law which prohibits discrimination on the basis of race, religion, age or sex where employment is concerned. Many states also have fair employment practice laws.

As a retailer, a small business man, you'll have to know about the laws I have just discussed. In general, they cover industrial accidents, occupational diseases, involuntary unemployment, the provision of hospital and medical care and retirement incomes. Workmen's compensation laws cover industrial accidents and occupational diseases, and they vary considerably from state to state, so you'll have to consult local sources. Both state and federal laws cover unemployment benefits. The Social Security Act also requires employers to make a separate payroll calculations for the financing of hospital and medical care for those age 65 or over, as well as income to be paid after retirement.

Most retailers of the kind I've been talking about in this book are not going to be in interstate business, but if for some reason you are, be sure to consult federal authorities about the laws governing such activities.

Taxes

Now, let's turn to an even more painful subject—taxes. With the help of your lawyer, accountant and/or tax expert, you should investigate your tax situation before you start out in business. Your business will be taxed—and taxed. Federal taxes will include social security taxes shared with your employees, excise taxes and, if the business is incorporated, corporate income taxes. Various deductions have to be made from your employees' wages for old-age, survivor's, hospital and medical insurance taxes, besides unemployment compensation contributions, payment for the employees' individual federal income taxes, and state and local income taxes, if any.

If you happen to be a sole proprietor or a partner, you'll have to prepay your personal income taxes or keep them current on a quarterly basis. You can set up retirement plans for both yourself and your employees under the Self-Employed Individual Tax Retirement Act. The local office of the Director of Internal Revenue will be more than happy to give you information about your federal tax obligations, and the IRS also puts out a booklet entitled *Tax Guide for Small Business,* which is revised every year.

State and local taxes, including such common levies as income, property, sales, occupation or business license taxes and unemployment compensation taxes must be paid. State and local offices will advise you of your obligations. When you've compiled all the tax information you need—federal, state and local—you should draw up a worksheet setting all the taxes down, and when they come due. That way you'll know at a glance what you have to pay.

Insurance

Finally, there's the matter of insurance. Before you open your doors, you must be adequately covered or you stand to lose your investment. There is insurance for "acts of God" such as flood and windstorm and others for liability judgments and death of key personnel. Your insurance coverage should include fire, general liability, automobile liability, automobile physical damage, workman's compensation, crime, business interruption, glass, business life (on your key people), group life, group health and disability. It should *not* include insurance against losses that would not be important, or protection so expensive it amounts to a substantial part of the insured property's value.

As I've said earlier, you need to consult a good insurance agent, or broker, making the selection with considerable care. People in business will be good advisers on this point, since they've had dealings with many agents. You want an agent who will be able to supply all the coverage you need, who is known to be a highly competent professional, and who is willing to devote time to your problems. He should be able to go over your whole situation and advise you about alternative methods of coverage.

In short, there are important laws, regulations, taxes and insurance problems you need to know about, to the extent of being able to find competent help who will allow you to feel reasonably secure on these matters.

10

Buying and Selling

IN EARLIER CHAPTERS I've talked about buying and selling in a general
way, and given some specific information about the kind of merchandise beginners should stock. But since the art of buying and selling is,
obviously, what the retail business is all about, there are many other
things a novice should know, and I'm going to cover as many of them
as possible in this chapter.

How To Buy Wisely

First, some information about buying. Many new retailers have gone
out of business because they bought unwisely, and consequently never
had a chance to find out whether they could really sell. Experience
may be the best teacher here, but a few tips may make the learning
process easier and less expensive.

It pays to determine your sources of supply very early in the game.
Not only should you know what's being offered, and how much it's
going to cost you and on what terms, but also how fast the supplier is
going to be able to get it to you. Subscribe to trade magazines that
serve your field and consult their advertisements; the best suppliers
will almost certainly be advertisers.

As I said earlier, the name brands are best when you can get them, and almost indispensable for the beginner. Put aside your personal preferences when it comes to buying in favor of items that have proved to be sellers. Take your time and ask questions. If it's possible, first test an item with a small order before you go into larger figures. Keep your inventory low at the beginning, otherwise you'll be tying up a lot of your money if some items happen to move slowly. If it's an established business, don't be in a hurry to change the buying pattern until you've operated it for a time. Don't be afraid of running out of stock; a good supplier can reach you quickly. And finally, be sure you know the meaning of that important word, "keystone," which you'll see in the catalogs and price lists. It separates cost price from selling price, and means that the cost price is 50 percent of the listed price.

As for what name brands you should carry, I can only say, "Get the best." I carried the highest quality luggage and small appliances when I began E. J. Korvette. Selling secondary merchandise—that is, unfamiliar brands not pre-advertised—simply won't work; customers will be far more difficult to sell and to satisfy. It only makes sense to sell what is pre-sold by the manufacturer.

The problem of inventory is always important, and sometimes troublesome. For any particular category of merchandise—jewelry, for example—there will usually be statistics available on sales volumes for various kinds of goods. By studying them, you should be able to estimate what your store can sell.

Knowing *what* to buy is also a large part of the game. Often you can rely on salesmen and wholesalers' representatives, but you'll have to keep a sharp eye out for the high-pressure types who will sell you anything they can. Most of them, however, would rather have you as a good, satsified and steady customer, and their experience can be of help to a new retailer. After a while, experience will tell you what you should buy to satisfy local buying needs. The income of the customers will be a large determinant in this respect, but remember that even customers with high incomes like low-priced goods and bargains.

Customers are inclined to be fickle, though—their preferences are subject to quick changes which you'll have to get used to. A big promotion for a particular product can change these preferences almost overnight. Such shifts make it impossible for any buyer to be right all the time. Some stock will always fail to sell as well as expected.

You can hold these misjudgments to a minimum simply by keeping your eyes open to what's going on and following changing demands closely. That's another advantage of name brands. The demand for them is relatively constant, since they're always well advertised and people know them. It's the new products you'll have to be careful about, particularly cosmetics and toiletries, where customer preferences are often seasonal. If you live in a small town, you should remember that

promotional campaigns carried out in large cities and in national publications may not have an impact on your community for two months
or more after they have been felt in metropolitan areas.

One lesson every retailer learns is to watch his competition closely—they're watching you, too. If someone else is doing better business
than you are, there has to be a reason. And expect to be imitated
whenever you're successful.

A useful tool in your equipment for retailing is a "want book,"
which lists items you need to buy so that you won't run out of stock.
Automatic reordering is risky because it doesn't take changing conditions into account; the want book solves that problem. Order what you
need, *when* you need it.

How Much To Buy

How much to buy depends on your understanding of what turnover
means. Briefly, it's the number of times your inventory is sold and
replaced within a given period of time—the ratio of the cost of goods
sold to the average inventory. The inventory itself is, of course, a
periodic physical counting of your stock and determining its worth
based on current market prices.

There are a few pitfalls here. For example, high turnovers are not
necessarily a good thing. They may come from carrying too low an
inventory in relation to sales, which means you are probably running
out of stock often and consequently losing customers. On the other
hand, the higher the rate of turnover, the less capital you will be compelled to invest in inventory.

When the turnover rate falls below average in your business, it's
time to find out why. Are your competitors doing something you're not?
Maybe the inventory remains stable but sales are decreasing, or purchases are too far ahead of sales. It may be that inventory should be
decreased temporarily to conform to sales trends. Perhaps the inventory itself should be examined to see if it contains too many items that
can't be sold.

If you're running a business with several departments, remember
that you've got more than one turnover rate to worry about—the one
for the whole store, and one for each department. If one of those
departments is turning over only once a year, no doubt it should go.
Another department may be showing an increased turnover rate, and if
there's someone in it who's responsible, he or she is worth holding on to
and perhaps promoting.

When you are able to measure your turnover rates accurately,
you'll be able to forecast your purchases and sales. In measuring them,

and analyzing them later, look for the causes of slow turnover: there may be too many brands or sizes, or too high prices or price schedules. Maybe you're buying too much at a time, or from too many sources. Colors and materials may be wrong. Articles may be shopworn. Perhaps you haven't discovered what your customers really want. Often it's a case of salespeople who don't know the stock, and aren't interested enough to find out. Maybe you haven't been taking inventory often enough, or your stock control records are deficient. And it may be you haven't planned adequately for seasonal changes.

Whatever the reasons for slow turnover, they need to be discovered and corrected at once, because a high turnover will give you several advantages. For instance, you'll need less storage space and shelf room, which means you'll have more room for display and you'll be able to take on more items. Further, there won't be so much dead stock on hand that will either have to be sold for little profit or thrown out. Finally, and probably most important, you won't have too much capital tied up in unsold stock, so there'll be more money that can be put to work for you elsewhere. All of this can mean the major difference between profit and loss.

When To Buy

As you can see, buying is a good deal more complicated a matter than it appears. You will be making decisions constantly, about what to buy, from whom to buy it, when to buy it, and how much to order. You may want to spread out your buying among several suppliers to get more favorable prices and to take advantage of whatever promotions are being offered at any one time. It may be better, however, to stick with as few suppliers as possible. You'll get more attention and help, there will be a smaller investment in inventory and your larger purchase orders will mean larger discounts. Credit problems will be simplified. On the whole, fewer seems better. I might add that credit terms vary from 30 to 60 or 90 days. On the average, most small businesses are able to get 60 days.

As for when to buy, the seasons determine this. But there are other factors, too, such as taking advantage of prices that may be temporarily low. Remember, though, this is speculative buying, and like any speculation, subject to risk of loss. In the matter of how much to buy, the answer is less complicated: Don't overbuy. Between careful analysis of your records and the good judgment you develop with experience, that needn't happen.

All your buying problems will be helped by keeping records—stock control particularly, in terms of both dollars and physical units. The dollar controls will tell you how much money you have invested in every category of merchandise. Unit controls tell you what individual items you have available.

Pricing

Overhead is a key factor in pricing. The ordinary markup should cover expenses, leaving enough for your own return plus interest on your invested capital. Be consistent about your markup and don't think you have to sell for less just because you'll lose a customer. A common mistake is to think that a profit, any profit, in hand is better than letting a customer get away without a sale. It isn't so. Following this policy can lead to bankruptcy. In the case of loss leaders—those items marked down to attract people to the shop and to other goods—be sure that they are items in great demand or the sacrifice won't be worth it. Beware, too, of meeting discount competition by flamboyant merchandising responses, featuring perpetual "giant sales," "closeouts" and "drastic price reductions." It's a sure way to lose credibility with the public.

Pricing is highly important to your operation, and it is astonishing how many beginning retailers fail to understand the relationship between accurate pricing and profitable sales. You will have a general price policy, of course, when you go into business, but you will have to price the individual items so that you can make a profit. Let's look at this a little more closely.

"Markup" and "gross margin" are words often used interchangeably. Both mean the spread between what merchandise costs and what it sells for. That difference has to cover every expense except the cost of the merchandise, and also the profit on your investment. A markup is customarily expressed as a percentage of the selling price, or sales, not of the cost. The cost percentage and the markup therefore add up to 100 percent of the selling price. Knowing the cost and the markup, you can find the price by dividing cost by the cost percentage.

In applying the markup, there's a difference between theory and practice. For example, if your expenses are 30 percent of your gross receipts and you expect a 4 percent profit on sales, you should be able to apply a 34 percent markup to every item. Not so. It may take more time and persistence to sell some goods, and items occupy varying amounts of space. Both turnover and depreciation rates vary. It's better to establish markups by departments, merchandise categories, or both, and even then you won't be able to apply them uniformly.

Customers have become fairly sophisticated about prices, and while they respond to various kinds of sales designed to get people into a store, in many cases they don't accept what's offered to them at face value. Low prices attract them, but reasonable prices keep them coming back.

If you're going to cut prices across the board, remember that you will also have to cut costs at the same time, or else generate a high enough sales volume to compensate for reduced profit margins. It's also advisable to avoid too much "cut price" advertising; many people believe that you get only what you pay for. A customer is most impressed with a purchase when he sees the reduced price clearly stated below the list price.

How To Sell

The literature on salesmanship would fill the shelves of the New York Public Library, and it increases every year. So much has been written on the subject that maybe we've forgotten the simple basics.

How do you sell? Directly, by means of your own efforts with a customer. Indirectly, by advertising and direct mail, through display and packaging. Your attitudes and behavior toward the general public play an important part.

As you will discover, establishing a business of your own means there will be a lot of people to whom you'll have to sell—customers, bankers, suppliers, among others. Take a hard look at your own capabilities. If you're not a first-class salesperson yourself, get an associate who is or your chances for success will be minimal.

In retailing, whether you succeed or not depends largely on your familiarity with what you're selling, your own qualities of salesmanship, your knowledge of the customers you serve and your personal manner with others. In the end, it's the customers who are the most important factor. Study them. Good salespersons are good psychologists. They learn how to listen to the customer as well as how to question him or her.

As I've said earlier, I was a very good salesperson, and aside from whatever natural talents I had, I'm sure that one of the reasons was my complete involvement in every facet of the business. That kind of participation generates a following among the people with whom you are dealing. I believe this principle applies just as much to retailers starting out today as it did to me two decades ago. Customers had confidence in me, and since I knew that I was selling the best, it was both easy and pleasurable to be sincere in my sales presentations.

Every book on salesmanship dwells, with justice, on one important fact: The salesperson must be careful about what he or she says. Most often quoted is the observation of the supersalesman, Elmer Wheeler, who wrote: "Your first 10 words are more important than your next 1,000." The approach should be made with care, remembering that customers recoil from exaggeration and what they perceive as only half-truths. They don't like to be argued with, neither do they like being asked to make a decision before they're ready. Some retail salespersons think the sale is over when the decision to buy is made. It isn't. From the customer's viewpoint, it's over when he gets his change and leaves. If what happens in between is perfunctory, or if he is ignored, he isn't likely to be a repeat customer.

A retailer should study his products as well as his customers. It goes without saying that the salespeople on the floor should know the stock thoroughly, but the owner should know it as well or better. He should know what his customers are finding most appealing about it, how it is best used or, if it's a new product, what makes it special. All this information has to be conveyed to the customer by the salespeople. They are only expected to know this about the products they're selling in their particular department. The owner should know all about everything he has in stock.

Demonstrations, if possible, help a customer who's buying a product for the first time. Explanations are also useful if you're trying to persuade the customer that it's more economical for her to buy larger quantities of an item than she might ordinarily buy—toothpaste, for example. Trying to tie-in some other related product to a sale is dangerous unless it's done subtly; customers *don't* appear to object, however, if it's something unrelated.

Don't knock what you don't sell, and *don't* downgrade your competitors. Concentrate on what you do have, and on your own business. If you've bought someone else's business, it's equally dangerous to criticize the former owner. You never know when you're talking to a loyal customer at the store. Try to improve on the former owner's performance and let people see what you are without verbally drawing any comparisons.

Use complaints to advantage. To respond with hostility to an angry customer is to lose one. It is much better to treat the situation as an opportunity to learn something about your business from someone who doesn't like it and is more than willing to tell you why Marshall Field I, one of the greatest drygoods retailers in history, is credited with coining the slogan, "The customer is always right." His great Chicago store was built on that principle, and time hasn't proven him wrong.

11

Selecting and Training Personnel

UNLESS YOU'VE STARTED A SOLO OPERATION, one of your first tasks as a retailer will be selecting and training the people who are going to work for you. Even if you start out in a small way, with only family members or partners to help, soon the time will come, if the business is successful, when you'll have to deal with the personnel issue.

Many people going into business make the initial mistake of not being clear in their own minds about what they want their new employees to do. In a small business you need people who are flexible to do a lot of things—just as we did in the first E. J. Korvette store on Forty-sixth Street. Therefore you should build the kind of organization you need from the beginning. Write down the job descriptions for the personnel you require and then, when you're hiring, simply look for the people who can best fill your needs.

Sources of Personnel

There are several sources to scout. Your friends, business acquaintances and associates will be the primary sources. Others are the nearest United States Employment Service Office; placement bureaus in high schools, business schools and colleges; trade and industrial associations, employment agencies, want ads in local newspapers—and, always, the people who come in looking for jobs.

Screening applicants can be done by asking them to fill in personnel forms, but nothing can replace the personal interview. Eventually, when your business is big enough, you'll have a personnel office doing that work, but in the beginning you should to it yourself, and do it thoroughly. The best way is to begin by describing your business in general and the job in particular, then let the applicant talk about herself.

When the applicant has told you all she can, ask questions. It's important to know everything you can about her. Check references, too; some employers are inclined to neglect this part of the hiring process. But when you do, use them as a check primarily against what the applicant has told you. Much of the rest you'll hear will be subjective judgments which may or may not be true.

After an employee is hired, provide enough training time as well as on-the-job experience with close supervision before evaluating his or her performance.

Working with Your Employees

The Small Business Administration recommends a Human Relations Program for businesses, but whether you elevate it to the status of a program or not, efficient and productive employees are certainly determined by the human relations effort of the employer and his associates.

People have physical as well as psychological needs. As an employer, you can't do anything about the physical needs of your employees except to provide the money that will satisfy them. Psychologically, however, the way you treat them has a great deal to do with how well they work for you. Remember, the primary psychological need is to be accepted; the second is to be recognized.

To help your employees satisfy their needs, you should make a real effort to understand your workers from the beginning. A major obstacle to understanding is the belief that actions have single causes—for example, the notion that neatly dressed people are orderly in other things, or that students with mediocre grades are likely to do mediocre work at the next stage in their lives. It's dangerous to generalize about behavior. Look for what's under the surface in each human being with whom you're dealing, and most of all, keep in mind that genuinely caring for your employees can be as important in the long run as caring about your mordise and store.

Do everything you can to make people feel they're important on the job. That doesn't mean giving excessive flattery or treating employees as though they were children. It does mean communicating to them exactly what the rules and regulations are, how your business is structured, and what constitutes the chain of command. Employees should know exactly what their responsibilities and duties are, and these should be equally understood by their superiors and co-workers. If things aren't clear, people become defensive, and when they're defensive, the next step is dissatisfaction and all that goes with it. Increased productivity almost inevitably follows when employees believe their employer is honestly concerned about their welfare.

The idea is to fulfill your employees' needs so that they will be motivated toward fulfilling the needs of the business. To do that, you'll have to keep reminding yourself that although the business may fill all your waking thoughts and occupy your dreams as well, your employees have other concerns, and they are not impersonal working machines. Their personal concerns—most often health, or family, or money—are important to them.

Employees need to feel, too, that they are accomplishing something in their work, and a wise employer will make them feel that the quality and quantity of their work are important. How well the employer succeeds in meeting his employees' needs is the primary determinant of how they perform their duties. It's much less expensive to diagnose a dissatisfied worker's attitude, find out what's causing it, and do something about it than it is to hire and train someone new. People who don't have favorable attitudes toward their work, don't do their best. They want to be treated like people, not like part of the equipment.

It's just as important to understand groups as it is to understand individual workers. For example, if you asked 20 people in a business establishment what was the single most important factor keeping them happy on the job, they'd tell you it was the money. But if you analyzed the members of this same group when they left their jobs to take another, you'd find that money was not the only reason, and often not the most important one.

What makes for good attitudes on the job among groups of people? A major university has made a series of studies on this question, and the results may surprise you. First on the list is security, as far as the morale of the group is concerned. Interest comes second, followed by opportunity for advancement, appreciation, company and management, and the intrinsic aspects of their job. This is followed by money—only seventh on the list, supervision, the job's social aspects, working conditions, communication, hours, ease and benefits. It's interesting to note that the considerations most often heard around the bargaining table in labor negotiations come rather far down on the list.

Every study shows that supervision is a major factor in employee morale and job satisfaction. Again, the supervisor ought to be a person oriented toward the employees, who knows how to make them feel wanted and needed. If an employer thinks an employee is incompetent and doesn't care about his work, and acts that way toward him, the employee is likely to justify that opinion, no matter how good a worker he may really be. But if you treat him as though he were doing a good job and had the potential to do an even better one, there's a good chance he'll fulfill that expectation. The old-fashioned attitude toward employees was to treat them like children, and the result was the rise of powerful labor unions that treated employers with hostility and suspicion.

A Human Relations Program

No two businesses are alike, but it's still possible to institute a program for improving human relations in your own enterprise, by adapting whatever parts of a recognized general program fit your particular situation. That program should include the following:

Begin with improving your own understanding of human behavior, and accepting the basic fact that other people may not see things as you do. You'll have to recognize that someone else may sometimes have the right answer—even though you own the place.

Let your employees know you're interested in them, and solicit their ideas.

Treat them as individuals, and never impersonally.

Respect opinion differences, and whenever you can, explain why you're taking an action.

Help your employees with anything affecting their security.

Do whatever you can to make jobs interesting, and encourage promotion from within.

Give employees public recognition for jobs well done.

If you have to criticize, do it privately and constructively.

Train your supervisors to be as concerned as you are, and be sure the staff is informed on matters affecting them. Correct information is the best way to stop office rumors.

Adopt as your motto two simple words: Be fair.

Supervisors should get the same kind of treatment. Work with them, take them into your confidence, encourage cooperation, educate them in your and the company's goals, inform them of both your

short-range and long-range plans, make the lines of authority absolutely clear, give them clear-cut decisions, see that their status is suit-
ably recognized and pay them well. If you do all these things, you will
have a minimum of trouble.

In my own case, I created an atmosphere at E. J. Korvette in
which the employees were like a family. In the early days, they were
people I had known either in school or in the Army, so it was even
easier then to establish that kind of ambiance. We had a naturally
close relationship, and the cooperation was incredible. If it was necessary to work an 80-hour week, no one complained, and in those days
that was very often the case. I admit that those were unusual circumstances, but I tried to maintain that kind of relationship as the
organization expanded, and I believe it was accomplished with some
success. By following the program I've outlined above and adapting it
to your particular operation, I'm sure you can be successful too.

12

Selecting Your Suppliers

WHEN THE TIME COMES TO ORDER INVENTORY for your new business, you'll probably find yourself purchasing most of your stock from a few key firms. As I've recommended in previous chapters, order merchandise catalogs and call or visit the appropriate distributors and talk to the sales managers. You can trust their advice because the more you sell, the more they'll sell. This would also be the proper time to pin down exactly what their credit terms are going to be. Wholesalers usually don't sell on consignment, but if you're just getting started, they may make exceptions.

If it's possible, you should try to find a wholesaler able to supply from 60 to 80 percent of your needs. It's not likely that you'll find one who can supply you with everything. For the remaining 20 to 40 percent, seek out specialty wholesalers.

What do you look for in a wholesaler? Here's a checklist:

He should be a dependable source of quality merchandise, one who will be able to guide you in picking out what you should have.

He should be able to deliver goods to you at prices that will enable you to sell competitively, although there will be times when he won't be able to meet competition on certain items. Consequently, it's a waste of time to try to compare prices on every item.

He should be able to handle your orders rapidly and competently, at least 85 percent of the time. Anything less means that you're losing money. It adds to your cost of doing business if he sends you incorrect items, wrong sizes or wrong brands, so check on him constantly to see how well he fulfills your orders.

Be sure your wholesaler is one who sincerely wants to help you, not just talk about it. Performance counts here.

Kinds of Wholesalers

You may be surprised to know that there are several different kinds of wholesalers. There are, to begin with, the old-line or full-functioning wholesalers, and they're the best bet for the kind of retailing I've been advocating in this book. They usually stock full lines of name-brand merchandise, and they sell to retailers, calling directly on stores. This kind of wholesaler may have some sales aids to offer, but primarily he's in the business of providing you with a steady supply of saleable merchandise. They are usually financially solid houses, and so will be able to offer you the most liberal credit as a regular retail customer. You'll never be asked to limit the size of your order, nor will you be told when to place it. I always dealt satisfactorily with these conventional full-line wholesalers, whose salespeople called on accounts, and I recommend them.

Another kind of operation is known as the program wholesaler. Retail customers sometimes share in their ownership. They stock name brands, but they also carry private label goods under the wholesaler's own brand. The program wholesaler will probably offer you one of two plans, either his full line at regular prices if he's going to be only a source for merchandise, or if you join his "program," you'll be asked to buy specified quantities of certain goods. With this, of course, come rebates, identification and sales aids. Often these program wholesalers are in league with similar, noncompeting wholesalers elsewhere in the country. It's a kind of operation that seems to be increasing.

Still another operator is the franchise wholesaler, whose emphasis is on management and merchandising guidance for the stores he franchises. You won't have to invest in the parent company, in most cases, but if you take the franchise you will find yourself under a strict buying and stock control plan and in some cases will even be told exactly how to lay out your store. You'll also have to buy most of your merchandise from a central warehouse, and use a certain quantity of circulars and promotional materials every year. You'll have to decide whether you think the sales and management assistance you get is worth the stringent controls. There are fees involved in franchising, varying from one franchise to another.

Then there are the wholesalers owned by groups of dealers. To join the group, you'll have to invest some money in the company, and will probably be required to buy annually about $50,000 worth of wholesale merchandise, ordering on forms supplied by the company. You may also be required to order certain kinds of merchandise at specific times. These wholesalers can operate at a 10 percent markup or less because they eliminate salespeople, deal only with large-volume retailers and reduce to a minimum their internal paperwork and merchandise handling. Obviously, if you're not yet a large-volume retailer this situation is not for you, but it's something to keep in mind as your business grows. The dealer-owned wholesalers handle mostly private label merchandise, and their primary effort is to establish a good retailing outlet in every major marketing area. Starting in the Midwest, these establishments have branched out to other parts of the country and operate only in particular retail fields.

Specialty wholesalers, as their name implies, don't try to fill all your needs, but only provide merchandise in their or specialized categories. If your business has several departments, at least one or two of them can best be supplied by a specialty house, particularly if you are trying to develop a big potential with one of them. In any case, consider these people as a valuable secondary source of supply.

Finally, in some cases you may find it advisable to buy directly from manufacturers, some of whom make only direct sales. Remember, there's one disadvantage in this: you'll probably have to order larger quantities than you would from a wholesaler. That means you're tying up inventory cash, and creating the need for more storage space.

So, to sum up, which wholesaler should you select? Concentrate your business as much as you can in a single wholesaler, because you'll get more consideration and attention that way. If you spread your orders around you may save a little on individual items, but you will inevitably add to your buying costs. Before you decide, analyze your operating plans and pay particular attention to your gross sales and your location. Don't consider a dealer-owned group unless your sales are large enough to take advantage of the discounts it offers. A franchise operation may be the answer if you have so little experience that the ready-made help you'll get from one is worth it to you. For the retailer just starting out, I'd recommend the old-line, full-functioning wholesaler. But in any case, whatever kind of wholesaler you choose, be sure that it's one who will give you a competitive advantage.

13

Store Planning and Layout

In earlier chapters I talked about store planning in specific terms for the particular stores I recommended starting. In this chapter, I want to discuss planning and layout from a more general standpoint, for the benefit of those who may want to start some other kind of store.

Planning begins, of course, as soon as you find the premises suitable for your needs. You'll be ordering equipment and supplies based on the physical set up and the inventory of the store, as well as the ideas you have with respect to what you want your store to look like.

The first step is to get it all down on paper. From this will come your long-range plans, adjusted from time to time to accommodate new ideas and customer demands. Don't underestimate the importance of presenting your stock as attractively as you can. If it's done effectively, experts estimate you can add from 15 to 25 percent to your total sales.

If you haven't planned your store well, it will probably be reflected in poor business. Should you find yourself in that position sometime after you've opened your store, it may help to look at it with a fresh eye one morning, as though you were a customer instead of the owner. Ask yourself these questions:

Would I shop here if I happened to be going by?

Would I be turned off by faded or disorderly window displays, or cluttered ones that jumble the merchandise together?

How would I find a particular item if I came in here to look for it?

Is the light strong enough to find things?

Are individual categories separated and clearly marked?

Is it easy to find the prices?

After that kind of examination, it may help to compare your store with another nearby that appears to be doing a brisk business, using the same criteria listed above. Often the contrast is extremely informative.

At the beginning, a great deal of trouble can be avoided if you take the time to analyze your objectives, and figure out how to get the most value from every square foot of your floor space. To do that, you'll have to devise a plan that will increase and maintain the flow of traffic through your store.

It isn't an easy job, and if you feel doubtful about doing it yourself, there are professional store planners who will do it for you—for a fee, of course. But the main thing is to be sure at the start, before any planning is done by anybody, that you know exactly where you're going, in detail, and why. Don't forget that the prime consideration is your customers. You're designing the store for them, and the object is to attract them and then make it easy for them to shop. Everything else should revolve around that concept.

Here is a list of do's and don'ts to help with your planning:

First figure up the costs, whether the premises you're moving into are new or will have to be modernized.

Get the figures for the lights and electric outlets you'll require, including whatever rewiring that may be needed.

Find out whether the flooring is adequate or needs to be repaired, or possibly replaced.

Check heating and ventilation to see if they are adequate.

Determine whether your store is big enough and your customers numerous enough to warrant installing a telephone booth.

Check to see if the water supply is adequate for your own office needs, and possibly for the customers if the store is large enough to require rest rooms.

Don't get carried away and buy more equipment and fixtures than you really need. They're expensive.

Before you buy each unit, ask yourself whether it will really sell more merchandise and whether it presents your stock to best advantage.

Decide whether your equipment and fixtures are going to be uniform in finish, color, height and style. Maybe you'll need special installations; these will be an additional expense.

If you have self-service counters, be sure the shelves are at the proper height and not so deep that you'll have to have them constantly well filled, thus increasing your inventory.

Once you've done the original planning, you can sit down with a sheet of squared paper and draw an outline of your selling floor space to scale, showing the doors, windows, shafts, columns, stairways, radiators, light fixtures, electrical outlets and anything else that may be involved in the layout. Then, using another sheet, draw in your fixtures and equipment, including counters, display cases, shelving, gondolas and whatever else you plan to use as fixtures. By drawing them to scale and pasting them on cardboard, you can cut them out and place them on your floor plan to find out exactly how things are going to look. In this way you can experiment with layouts, moving the units around until you have what you want. Then you can paste the equipment and fixtures onto the floor plan and you'll have a graphic representation of how the store will look. You could have an artist do all this, of course, but you'll learn more by doing it yourself.

Be careful not to clutter your plan. The basic design of many successful stores today is the use of open space to draw customers farther inside. Aisles are the arteries of your store. Be sure that the blood (that is, the customers) is able to flow through them freely without overcrowding. Aisles ought to be from 42 to 60 inches wide, and kept clear. The flow should be from the front to the back of the store, with the impulse items at the front and demand items at the rear, which may be subtly spotlighted to draw further attention. At least one section of the front space should be flexible enough so that you can use it for special promotions. In all cases, leave yourself room enough to operate.

One expert has listed six pitfalls to watch out for in organizing sales space. Here they are:

Be sure to decide on definite and practical objectives.

Make and follow a comprehensive written outline of the program.

Overcome your inexperience by using the advice of experienced and reliable experts.

Don't copy others without checking their results.

Don't be too economical.

Be sure you're not another victim of delay and procrastination, two of your chief enemies.

Perhaps one more rule should be emphasized. *Design your store so that it looks like the kind of operation it's supposed to be.* You wouldn't lay out a drug store so that it looked like a supermarket, or vice versa. Each kind of store has its own aspect to present to the customers, and the design in general should conform to it. This doesn't mean, obviously, that every grocery store and every drug store should look alike. They should clearly express their own nature and purpose and at the same time achieve a healthy degree of individuality.

14

Promotion and Advertising

THE BIGGEST DAY OF YOUR RETAILING LIFE will be the day you open your new store. All the planning I've been talking about up to now is going to be subjected to the first real test—getting people into the place.

My own experience with the first E. J. Korvette store won't be much help here. If you remember, we simply made ourselves known to the people who worked in the buildings in our area, through their supervisors and personnel staff, and waited for the knowledge of our values to spread by word of mouth. Later, when we were operating large stores, we hired advertising and promotion professionals to saturate the media with ads.

In our original store on Forty-sixth Street our only street-front space was three rather small windows on the second floor with gold lettering to describe the character of the store—luggage and small appliances. Laying out the place was equally simple. We visited a few similar stores for comparison, solicited advice from our merchandisers, and went ahead on our own. We couldn't afford the professional store planners who do this kind of work for a fee. Today, far more sophisticated means are available to most beginners than the limited resources I had, and these are what I'm going to describe.

Helpful Hints for Opening Day

Suppliers are the first source of help you should look to. They've been through many openings with their customers, and their ideas can be extremely useful. Sometimes wholesalers offer you one or more of their salesmen to help you greet customers during the first few days. Their experience is reassuring to have available when the unexpected but inevitable bugs in your operation appear.

Since people like to get something for nothing, you may want to give away some kind of souvenir on your opening day to stimulate additional interest. Or, in some operations it may be possible to invite a celebrity connected with an item you're selling to greet the customers and sign records, books, or whatever tangible evidence of his fame you may be merchandising. If the store or the community is too small for that kind of thing, invite the mayor or some other local official who will be likely to get you some newspaper coverage as well. To help liven up the occasion, hire a model to hand out souvenirs or actually model clothes you're selling.

Direct mailings in advance of your opening will help to draw customers. They can simply go to boxholders in your postal zone, or if your store is one that deals in a specialty, you'll be able to buy a list of potential customers in your area from a list broker. Advertisements in local papers announcing the opening are almost essential, unless you're in a city so large that a small store's ad would be lost. In any case, look around your community, identify the people you wish to contact for the store's opening, and find the best way to reach them.

Depending on the kind of store you're opening, free soft drinks, or coffee and doughnuts, may be appropriate for opening day. Or you may be able to arrange for a special demonstration of a product you're selling. In other words, exercise your ingenuity and think of as many legitimate ways to attract people to your store on opening day as you can. It's going to be an event you'll remember; if you can make your customers remember it too, they'll be back.

Naming Your Store

There are other advertising and publicity problems to think about as you launch your new business. One is the name of your store. A drive down any city street will remind you of how much ingenuity goes into this exercise. There are probably going to be at least several stores in your community or general area that sell the same kind of merchandise you're retailing, so the task of having your store recognized begins with giving it a distinctive name. You should also give some thought to devising a trademark or logo for the store that can be used outside the building, on stationery, billing forms, and every other kind of printed material identified with your enterprise. It's worth getting a commercial artist to do the designing, and if the results seem good enough to protect, talk to your lawyer about registering your trademark. Once you have such a trademark, you can also build your advertising around it, using it in window displays and on shopping bags as well.

Window Display

Window display is important. Some retailers think it's the most important kind of advertising they do, because it's a direct link between the prospective customer and the store. If what he sees in the window persuades him to come into the store, he's likely to buy something whether it's an item he's seen in the window or not.

Many manufacturers will provide you with promotional materials for window display, including backgrounds, reprints of national advertising, dummy materials, and other aids—probably more than you can use (depending, of course, on the kind of business you're in). Some companies even offer window dressing services, either free or for a fee. Most new retailers want to dress the windows themselves, but not everyone has the talent to do this, and you may want to hire expert help unless you find someone with that ability among your first associates. There are freelance window-trimming services you can call.

Window dressing is an art in itself, carried to its highest peak in the artistic creations that appear every Christmas in the windows of great stores such as Lord & Taylor in New York. But on the level of the small retailer, the important thing to remember is that your windows are designed and dressed to draw people into the store. The displays must always be in the best condition, and they must be changed frequently.

Media Advertising

When it comes time to advertise, which will be almost immediately, you'll have to make up your mind which medium is going to be best for your store—newspapers, radio, television, direct mail or whatever approach is applicable to your specific needs. Part of the answer will be determined by cost. As a small retailer just starting out, you aren't likely to be able to afford television right away. But you might think about one minute or thirty-second commercials on the local radio station.

Most likely, however, your first advertising will be done in the local newspaper. The small retailer usually discovers that this is the best medium for him, particularly on a limited budget. Advertising experts will tell you that small ads run regularly get more business

over a period of time than large ads run only occasionally. The difficulty with small ads is making them stand out somehow from the other
advertising that threatens to bury them. It can be done, but again, you
may need some expert help unless you discover you have a talent for
laying out and writing distinctive advertising copy. A newspaper's
advertising department will assist you if necessary.

One way to rescue your small ad from oblivion is to get it placed in
the same location each time it runs, such as adjacent to a popular feature in the paper. Such a preferred location may cost you more money,
but it should be worth the additional expense. Some papers won't
charge extra if you contract to give them an ad for that space over a
long period of time. Some papers prefer to group the ads of small
retailers who are in the same business in one part of the paper, which
has its advantages because the large bloc of ads is an attention-getter.
But in that case, you'll have to work harder than ever to make your ad
stand out from the others. In the end, you can hope to have a business
large enough to justify hiring an advertising agency to do the work for
you. It costs more than doing it yourself, naturally, but most often it's
worth the expense.

Manufacturers in some industries offer cooperative ads to dealers,
and if that is the case with your particular kind of store, it will be an
extra help for you. The manufacturer pays part of the media cost of an
ad that features his product. On occasion, he'll even pay for the entire
ad, if a new product is being pushed. You'll save in another sense, too,
because manufacturers usually want you to use their stock ads for
cooperative advertising, thus saving you time and money. Only your
logo has to be added. If you insist on doing the ad yourself, they will
still supply the materials—photos, cuts, mats, proofs, and so on.

Other Media Saturation Points

A direct-mail campaign, an excellent way to introduce a new shop, can
also be a great means of continued publicity. It can be as simple as a
postcard, or as elaborate as a brochure or a catalog. Again, manufacturers often provide material you can use for these purposes. There are,
in addition, advertising companies which specialize in direct-mail
promotion, and if you can afford one of them, it's best to have such
specialists do the job for you. The major advantage of direct mail is
that nothing else is competing for attention when your potential customer is reading it, unlike any of the other media.

Other kinds of media besides the ones I've mentioned, such as car
cards, are inexpensive and useful ways to familiarize the public with
your store. The Yellow Pages telephone directory is a proven advertising medium. Commercial telephone subscribers are listed automatically, but it may be worthwhile to spend a little money and have your

shop listed in boldface, or even in a small display ad. Find out, too, whether the Welcome Wagon organization operates in your community; if it does, it's a good idea to work with them by making special offers to newcomers and inviting them to your store to get acquainted.

Your Advertising Budget

How much money should you budget for advertising? It depends on the kind of business you're operating, but it should be at least from 3 to 5 percent of net sales. The most important thing to remember about advertising is that it works best when it is continuous, and your budget should be tailored with that in mind. It's the regular daily ad that gets the best results.

In the end, it's not so much a question of how much money you budget for advertising as how you spend it, and there are a few basic rules that will prevent you from throwing your money away, as it's so easy to do:

> *Decide what kind of people you want as customers, and angle your advertising directly to them. Don't just invite everyone to the party and hope for the best.*
>
> *Decide on the store image you wish to create—what you want to be known for—and shape your advertising accordingly. You may want to be known for low prices, or for service and quality, or for items that are hard to get elsewhere.*
>
> *Use your distinctive logo in every ad; repetition is a basic principle in advertising.*
>
> *In local advertising, use material that supports industry promotional themes because national consumer advertising usually runs in connection with them and that will greatly help your local effort.*
>
> *Don't crowd your copy. White space gets attention too.*
>
> *Don't neglect planning. Beginning and inexperienced retailers often follow the easiest path, taking the first mat they see and giving it to the newspaper.*
>
> *Be flexible about your advertising plans—even if you've decided on a certain percentage of sales for your advertising budget, don't feel you have to spend that amount every month.*
>
> *Take advantage of any co-op plan you can get—if you don't, your competition will use them in the effort to get business away from you.*

You should tailor your advertising program to your own needs. There are so many ways to advertise, and so far I've only mentioned the best-known ones. You will want to look into store demonstrations, display signs, billboards, point-of-purchase racks, and other kinds of promotion and advertising. Look over the whole field, examine every approach, and then decide on what is best for your store and for the area in which you're doing business. Whatever you decide on, make a program on a day-to-day, month-to-month, year-to-year basis. It's the most effective way to get results.

15

Credit and Security

CREDIT IS AN INTEGRAL PART of our economic system, but if you're a new retailer, one of the first questions you're going to ask yourself is, "Can I afford to start selling on credit?" Important as it is, credit isn't for everyone. You may be preparing a financial trap for yourself if you start credit selling without estimating how much it will cost you to carry the accounts receivable. Unless you have a sound collection plan, you could experience credit losses as high as 20 percent—enough to guarantee bankruptcy.

True, selling on credit not only means increased sales volume, but also that you'll have to carry a larger inventory to accommodate your customers. The costs of handling credit transactions and billing must also be included in the overall cost. Some retailers who don't have savings as backing look for extra capital in the form of a bank loan, and there are several ways to go about acquiring loans. One is factoring, which means using your accounts receivable as collateral. Another possibility is long-term credit from manufacturers. All have peculiar advantages and disadvantages, and I recommend getting the advice of an expert before you take the leap.

Avoiding Credit Risks

There are risks in any kind of credit operation, and the problem is how to avoid them. Much of the trouble begins with the credit application itself. The retailer may be naive believing that most of the people who buy on credit intend to pay. There are some who find out they can't pay because of changed financial circumstances. The retailer needs to be strict with these people, for their good as well as his own. The number of people who accept credit knowing they are going to be delinquent is small, but numerous enough to give you trouble if you don't spot them. These professional delinquents usually know everything about credit. If you have any doubt at all about a customer who asks for credit, say no. It's the safest policy.

When someone applies to your store for credit, you can get a great deal of information from the applicant's credit references. Check them out carefully, and also be sure to see what information the local credit bureau has about the applicant before you decide. In the end, it's your experience and judgment that will most influence your credit decisions, but some retailers think it's a good idea to back themselves with a point system. They draw up a list of 10 or so characteristics of the good credit customer, then they rate applicants from 1 to 10 on each characteristic. The cutoff point comes at a predetermined number of points, and if the potential customer's score falls below that figure, credit is denied. Always remember that denial is your right, and so is the setting of standards. Credit is a privilege, not a right. If the possible loss of sales bothers you, remember that when credit is given and the bills aren't paid, your money is lost.

Not everyone should be billed at the same time. Good credit customers need to be billed only once a month; those with weak ratings should be urged to pay weekly or semi-monthly, thus pinpointing the delinquents early. Those who pay on time and regularly can be billed monthly later on, as proven reliable customers.

Since you're in the driver's seat, you can pick and choose the kind of credit customers you want simply by regulating your terms. A-dollar-down-and-fifty-cents-a-week brings one kind of customer; an entirely different group of people is attracted by tight terms and fast payment. You can't deal with everyone, so you'll have to pick your market and aim for it. As for those prompt payers whose accounts are closed, often the way to get them back to the store is to offer some kind of giveaway.

Billing and Collection

In the business of credit, billing deserves to be called an art, not a process that rests on simple principles. Consistency is the key word in any billing system. Bill customers consistently and systematically. Set monthly goals for collections, and see to it that you meet them. Check customers' credit statements every month. Separate them into groups of those who haven't paid for 30, 60 and 90 days, and you'll know at a glance how big a delinquency problem you have at any one time. If the delinquents are no more than 20 percent of your accounts receivable, the problem is in hand.

Collections should go on every day, with every late account prodded at least once a week, using a series of form letters. When the series runs out, it's time to get on the phone. Some customers will want to give you a partial payment, and you'll have to decide whether to accept it or insist on the full amount. The point is to be consistent and to have an overall system, rather than leaving collecting to chance.

Credit cards constitute another kind of credit business that has grown to extraordinary proportions in the last 25 years. There are great advantages to them for the retailer. The credit card companies take the risk and do the collecting. Moreover, your money will be tied up for a shorter time because these companies pay promptly. But you pay for such advantages, through the percentage fee the companies charge for their services. American Express, for example, charges 7 percent, while most of the others charge 4 percent. There's also the fact that you won't get any interest on installment accounts, and since the customer makes his payments directly to the credit card company or a bank in the business, you won't get the benefit of repeat traffic and direct contact.

Nevertheless, today it's a virtual necessity to accept all the major credit cards. We didn't do it in the beginning at E. J. Korvette only because they didn't exist in those days. As soon as credit cards came in, we accepted them because I could see that it was not only a necessity to stay in competition, but was also an asset in attracting customers who might go to a place where they could use their cards.

Don't forget about the Consumer Credit Protection Act when you extend credit. This "Truth-in-Lending" law applies to you unless payment in full is required in no more than four installments, and if no finance or other charges are made to the customer for using the credit plan. According to the law, you have to inform customers of every direct and indirect cost they will have to pay when they buy on credit, no matter how it's handled. The law also covers your advertising of credit terms. You must understand this legislation, which is enforced by the Federal Trade Commission. The free booklet, *What You Ought*

To Know about Federal Reserve Regulation Z, which you can obtain by writing to the Board of Governors, Federal Reserve System, Washington, D. C., 20551, will tell you what you need to know.

Problems of Security

As for internal checks on the handling of cash and collections in your organization, there are a few simple things you can do. Two independent employees should check all your cash and collections. Don't sign any checks until you see the bills and be sure you get a receipt for all cash transactions. Watch your mail receipts carefully; it's easy for cash to go astray. Petty cash payments should be recorded in ink and supported by vouchers which carry the date paid out or are otherwise marked so they can't be re-used. You may believe your employees are honest, and no doubt most of them are, but not everyone in promixity to money can resist temptation. These rules greatly reduce temptation.

Shoplifting, as I've said earlier, is always a problem and for many stores constitutes a major loss every year. There's no way to eliminate it completely. It can only be controlled by being sure that certain customers aren't left alone and unobserved, by being careful about what you put out on countertops within easy reach, and by watching every area of the store, particularly the front, where departing customers can be checked by experienced eyes. Even then, you can be sure that a certain amount of your annual loss figures can be attributed to pilferage.

The problem of whether to accept checks is a matter of policy every retailer has to decide for himself, weighing the risks against the advantage of accommodating good customers. If you accept them, it's common sense to insist on identification and make a note of it on the back of the check. If there are erasures or alterations on a check, don't cash it. Be sure the amounts shown on the check in both places are the same, and be particularly careful of personal checks which have unusually high sequence numbers. Many retailers won't take checks for more than the amount being purchased. Postdated checks shouldn't be accepted, and a check stamped "certified" doesn't guarantee its validity. Payroll checks should be treated as cautiously as personal checks, since professional check passers often print these on both real and imaginary companies. Finally, don't let the person with the check badger you into accepting it. If the signature isn't clear, ask how to spell the name and print it below the signature.

You should also take similar care with credit cards. Always compare the customer's signature on the sales slip with the signature on the card. If the card isn't signed, don't accept it until the customer proves it is his or hers by presenting other supporting identification.

Signatures in these cases are not sufficient proof of ownership of the credit card.

Security also means protecting your store against robberies both during and after business hours. Investigate the kind of alarm system that will best protect you at night and have it installed before opening your business. Inform the local police as to the kind of system you've installed so they will be on the lookout for any irregularities.

If you should be confronted by a robber during business hours, certain rules should be followed:

Never oppose the robber. Do whatever he tells you.

Study the robber carefully; try to memorize distinctive characteristics for later identification (height, weight, sex, age, color of hair, etc.).

If there is a getaway car, try to note its license number, model, color.

Call the police as soon as you can.

Preventive Measures

To combat the dangers we have just discussed, the store owner or manager must be continually on the alert. The precautions he must take may seem ridiculous to the average layman, but believe me, after being in the retail business almost all my life, they are necessary evils.

Store keys are to be kept on the owner's person at all times.

Employees' coats and handbags are not to be kept in merchandise selling area.

Employees' purchases are to be checked before they leave the store.

Before closing the store, check the safe to be sure it is locked. Check the rear doors, basements and dressing rooms.

If possible, never open or close the store alone. Make sure a trusted employee is present.

Employees should not leave the store without notifying the owner.

The owner must be present when garbage is disposed of.

Rear doors must be attended when open.

The owner should spend most of his time on the selling floor.

Incoming shipments must be checked accurately.

Mismarking of merchandise must be avoided.

Markdowns and markups of merchandise must be recorded accurately and on time.

Physical loss of merchandise due to unrecorded breakage must be avoided.

No employee is to ring up his own purchase.

Only an authorized person may handle refunds.

16

Your Competition

ONE OF THE FACTS OF BUSINESS LIFE is competition. It isn't necessarily a bad thing because where there's competition, there is a market and prospective customers. It is important, however, for you to know exactly what your competition is and how to compete within your specialty.

Let's say, for example, you're starting a retail camera store and will be selling camera equipment and related products, as well as developing film. Without even looking over the competition, you will be aware from your own experience that corner drugstores have made their photo departments into profitable parts of their businesses. Drug stores not only develop film on or outside the premises, but they also sell cameras and photographic equipment. Still, photography is usually a small adjunct to the drugstore's main business and won't offer you any formidable competition.

Department stores that have photo departments, owned or leased, are more threatening. The huge volume of a department store-run camera shop can often be attributed to highly capable salespersons who are most knowledgeable about cameras. However, and this is the case most often, the traffic that passes through this department is so congested that this is usually not the place for the novice camera bug to learn.

Your stiffest competitor will probably be the discounter. Most discounters offer the best name brands at big savings, but again, traffic through these stores prevents the salespersons from giving any kind of individual instruction to consumers.

As a specialty dealer, your best defense against competition is giving the customer personal attention—the kind that a large, busy discount store just isn't able to provide. As a specialty dealer, you can also expect help from some brand-name manufacturers, because they usually franchise their products and sell them through a limited number of agencies. Then, too, there are a good many items of equipment which a specialty store sells that a discount store won't handle. In this particular field—retail camera stores—many experts believe the gap between discount prices and those charged by the stores is constantly narrowing. This is chiefly because the discounters have been trying to give customers more informed service from their salespeople, and since that costs money, prices have risen. On the other side, retail camera stores have been going more into self-service, thus lowering overhead and prices.

You can also expect to get plenty of competition from other specialty camera stores in your area—and the same can be said of every other kind of retailing operation. One way you can cut down on your inventory and compete with the others is to make as many sales of major equipment as you can from catalogs instead of carrying the items in stock, taking advantage of the fact that you can usually get what you need from a supplier on short notice. Customers don't mind waiting if they get what they want at a savings. In short, you're cutting profits to make increased sales. The same thing can be done in other lines of retailing.

Another source of competition will be from the larger specialty camera shops, displaying a bewildering variety of items, advertising heavily, and drawing crowds of customers who generate the urge to buy among each other. You'll find these larger shops promote manufacturers' discontinued stock with closeouts at great reductions. Consequently, the prices in your shop may seem high. One way to combat this kind of competition is to carry franchised lines for which you're the exclusive dealer in your area. But once more, as in the struggle against discounters, your best bet is to give the customer the individual attention that the larger store cannot adequately provide. In the big store, the customer moves from one department to the other, from one clerk to another. In the small retail store, he or she gets one-stop, one-clerk service. There is no substitute for the personal touch—no matter what type of business you operate.

17

Keeping Records

IF THERE IS ONE AREA OF RUNNING A BUSINESS in which the new retailer is likely to be ill prepared, it's administration. Unless he's had management courses in college or some kind of formal training, he will have to rely on his innate talents, if he's lucky enough to have them. Not many beginners are that lucky, if we can judge by the number of business failures which are the result of inadequate and inefficient management. People who operate small businesses are compelled to make constant efforts towards improving their management skills, if they want to survive. Let's look at some of these management problems, especially record keeping.

Stock Control

First, let me emphasize how important it is to keep adequate stock records, as an indispensable aid to buying. These records will help you maintain well-balanced supplies of merchandise so that you'll be able to meet your customers' needs. They're also useful as a guide to forecast sales, to make your buying more effective, to generate greater profits, and to make it possible for you to hold down your investment in inventory.

There are several different stock control systems. Pick out the one you think is simple and complete as far as your business is concerned, and stay with it. Most of the systems provide a separate listing of every item in your store, by size or quality. The entry cards are also likely to list information about the supplier, the minimum order accepted, the terms, and similar matters. In any case, there should be spaces for purchase price, selling price, minimum supply, the quantity in stock, and the quantity on order. The materials for a stock control system are easily available in any large stationery or office supply store. You will probably find several kinds of systems available. They are all useful, and no one of them works any special magic. The one that will work best for you is the one you understand most fully.

At E. J. Korvette, we started out with the simple, basic accounting records, much as I've described here, including sheets for cash disbursements, receipts, a general ledger and so on. My friend Joe Zwillenberg, who began in the business with me, set up the original system, and we merely added to it as time went on and the business expanded.

Knowing when to reorder is a matter of determining your sales expectations for any individual item, and using your experience to allow enough time for delivery from your supplier. You should check on your minimum supply figures constantly.

Make one employee regularly responsible for keeping stock records in each department, or group of departments, routinely counting the stock every two weeks or so. Whenever an item seems to be getting down to its minimum level, he enters it in your "want" book, which you use in buying. When the order comes, he notes the increased quantity on his stock card. The stock cards themselves can be a "want" book if you like.

One clerk should make a check on incoming merchandise, comparing the quantity and kind of stock with the purchase order and the suppliers' invoice. If the supplier doesn't send his invoice until two days or so after the shipment, don't put the stock on the shelves until it gets there and you can check it. It's easier to pinpoint shipping errors that way, and it's also a protection in case the supplier's price has changed, which would mean that you'd have to alter your selling price.

Inventory

A general inventory needs to be taken at least once a year. The simplest way to do this is to hire an outside firm that specializes in this kind of work. They will put a crew into your store that will work nights until the job is done. If you adopt this method, be sure you're hiring an experienced firm that has a knowledge of your particular kind of business and whose crew members are individually bonded.

This is the worry-free but obviously expensive way to do inventory. Most retailers have their own employees do the job after store hours. You might want to follow these easy steps of taking inventory in your own store:

> Make a diagram of the store, showing every shelf and every part of your sales area and stockroom, divide it into sections, and assign your staff to the specific sections.

> Pair off your inventory takers—one persons counts while the other writes down the numbers. (If the staff is very small, one person will have to do both jobs, and in that case, he'll find he can work a great deal faster by using a tape recorder.)

> Give your staff complete information about when and how long you want them to work and what kind of overtime you intend to pay.

> Try to sweeten the pill by giving a post-inventory party.

Here are some ways to ensure a quicker and more accurate inventory count:

> *Have your stock arranged for easy, accurate counting.*

> *Be sure the people taking inventory know exactly what information they're supposed to obtain, and how you want them to do this, in terms of counting, pricing, listing, tabulating and checking.*

> *While the inventory is going on, spot check the counts on four or five shelves, checking quantity against listing.*

> *If there is a discrepancy, check it again to be sure before you challenge the inventory taker. You may be wrong. Even if you don't find any errors, the fact that you're making a spot check will make the inventory takers more conscious of the need for accuracy.*

> *If you can't complete the job before it's time to reopen the store, make allowance for goods sold from stock and for incoming shipments.*

An inventory, as I've said, is a valuable tool. Use it. Check and correct your stock control cards with it. Items out of stock may be disclosed, as well as odds and ends that ought to be liquidated by a special sale.

Cost Control

The inventory is only one way of controlling costs, which must be done if you hope to realize a profit. Financial records, carefully and accurately kept, are your best insurance that the costs *will* be controlled. It's essential to know how much your stock is costing you. Without that knowledge, you can't begin to cut costs, or even know whether it's possible. Do not, however, be so cautious about costs that you get yourself into a penny-pinching syndrome. Excessive cost control can hurt your business. Nevertheless, there are soft spots you should look for:

> *Make a careful check of your advertising program. If you don't get business as the result of advertising, you shouldn't be doing it or rather, you need to know why you aren't getting results. The ad may not be in the right newspaper at the right time, or maybe it should be done differently. Keep an ad scrapbook with notes of results; it will help you in your planning.*
>
> *Watch your interest and other bank charges. As municipal governments are discovering these days, interest charges can kill you if they're permitted to mount up. Keep an eye on what your loans and checking accounts are costing you. Accounts payable also have to be watched so that you don't miss the discounts. They can cut 2 percent or more from your stock prices.*
>
> *Keep a sharp eye on your cash register. People are sometimes careless about handling money. Even honest employees make mistakes if they're too casual about ringing up sales. If everyone knows that you're keeping track of your daily over and under figures, it will be a constant reminder to be careful.*
>
> *Charities need to be recorded carefully, not only for tax purposes but to be certain they are kept within reasonable limits, and directed towards purposes that will build good will. I'm talking specifically about business donations now, which should be dealt with accordingly; private contributions are a personal, not business, matter.*
>
> *Check into such matters as delivery vehicles to see that you're getting the best and most economical service from whatever trucker you're using.*
>
> *Insurance is a soft area. Some experts believe that many retailers could reduce their premiums 10 percent or more*

without significantly reducing their coverage. It's a good idea to review your insurance program periodically.

Store maintenance is a consideration because insufficient equipment, such as dirty air conditioners, will add to your expenses; this applies to everything else mechanical you may be using.

Markups require close examination. If your markups are based on incorrect costs—for example, by not including all your expenses—your profits will be cut. One-half of 1 percent of your annual gross is too high a figure to be careless about.

Give careful attention to refunds from suppliers, especially the credit given to you on refunds and returned stock.

Count accurately all the goods you return to distributors, and check your monthly statements every time.

Personnel can cost you money. A bad clerk may not only be getting more money than he's worth, but he's cutting into your profits by missing sales opportunities. The people you've hired aren't there to watch the store; their job is to sell, and you need to see that they do it. It's important to remember, too, that employee turnover is expensive when you consider training time and sales lost by inexperienced clerks.

It's easy to be careless about using supplies—add up their cost and you may be surprised by the results. The same principle applies to unnecessary use of lights, to personal telephone calls made by employees, and to equipment needlessly operated.

Keeping Accurate Records

Nothing you do in the direction of cost control will make much sense unless it is accompanied by accurate record keeping, as I hope I've made clear thus far in this chapter. I've talked about general principles in setting up a records system, now let's get down to some specifics.

The primary rule about keeping records is to be sure they are complete, simple, well organized, and up to date. Some records are required by law—payrolls, income and expenditures, and so on—but there are several others the retailer must keep. If you can possibly afford it, even when you're starting out on a slim budget, hire a good accountant to set up your records system and get it into operation (even part time). He's not only valuable in keeping records up to date, seeing that you make payments on time, including taxes, but he'll also be able to interpret figures for you, thus helping to keep costs down. If you can't afford an accountant, find out about the commercial record-keeping systems that are available, and pick out the one best suited to your business.

Sales slips are important records in any retail business. You should have an immediate written record of every transaction in your store that involves money or credit. Cash register receipts usually provide much of this information, but sales on account require sales slips. Customers want these slips, in case there's any problem with the merchandise, so it's a good idea to have your terms printed on the slips, covering completely the conditions of the sale. If you do direct-mail advertising, sales slips can also be a good source of names to add to your mailing list.

You should have an adequate supply of purchase orders in your shop; the printer will run them off or you can buy them at an office supply store. These forms should carry the purchase order number, your name and address, the vendor's name and address, the quantity of every item ordered, a description of each one, the selling price, the dealer net cost, and finally your signature at the bottom. Make out these orders in duplicate, with a carbon for your files. When you place a special order for a customer, clip a copy of his sales slip to your file copy of the purchase order. Orders placed by phone need a confirming purchase order, marked "confirmation," to prevent duplicate shipments.

There should be a regular procedure for receiving merchandise. Wherever possible, all merchandise should be received at one location, preferably a receiving platform. The following information should be entered on the receiving document:

> Name of vendor.
>
> Name of trucker.
>
> Trucker "pro" number.
>
> Date received.
>
> Freight charges, if any.
>
> Quantity of cartons.
>
> Signature of receiving clerk.

When merchandise is received, the stock clerk must do the following:

> Open shipment and remove packing slip or invoice.
>
> Check quantities listed against quantities received, and attach receiving report to packing slip or invoice.

If no packing slip or invoice is available, list quantities received and style numbers on copy of receiving report.

Check costs on invoice against purchase order.

Enter selling price from purchase order next to cost figure on packing slip or invoice.

Attach copy of receiving report to copy of purchase order and fill in either open or closed purchase order file, depending upon whether complete purchase order has or has not been received.

Attach duplicate copy of receiving report to packing slip and invoice and send to office for processing.

There is a procedure to be followed on bills payable. You should check the merchandise when it comes from the supplier against the packing memo and your purchase order. The cost of every item must be entered on the packing memo, which is filed alphabetically until the invoice arrives. When it does, compare it to the packing memo to be sure you're being billed for what you ordered at the price you agreed to pay. The invoice is then filed until you get the supplier's statement which summarizes your monthly purchases from him. Suppliers usually use the 25th of the month as the cutoff date for billing; anything bought afterward is billed the following month. Statements will reach you ordinarily about the first of the month, and payment is expected by the tenth, with 2 percent often deducted for prompt payment.

It's good sense to pay your bills on time, not only to get the discount but because it establishes you as a good credit risk with your suppliers. Besides, good customers (meaning those who pay on time) get preferred treatment when there's a shortage of supplies.

Staple all your invoices together when the monthly statement has been paid and file them for quick and easy reference. The year's invoices are transferred to an inactive file at the end of the year.

Another kind of record keeping is the inventory record. If you have many different items for sale, you'll probably keep detailed records only of major items. Use 5″ x 7″ cards and a file box. These cards should carry the name of the item, name of the supplier for each item, its serial number, date received, date sold, cost, selling price and, if you think the information can be used later, to whom it was sold. These cards will tell you at a glance what your stock situation is for any item, in addition to price changes and rate of sale. Your inventory records will be useful, too, in case you have to prove a claim for loss in a fire or burglary, so keep your file box in a safe or some fireproof container.

How to Profit from Accurate Record Keeping

These are the major kinds of records you'll be keeping—remember that you are going to need careful records to show your compliance with federal and state tax laws—not only your own tax returns but payments made by the business for social security and other deductions. They will also support your requests for credit from equipment manufacturers or from banks, and they will be very useful if you ever want to sell your business and need figures to substantiate your claims for it.

More importantly, you need records to help increase your profits. As the Small Business Administration points out, an adequate system will enable you to find the answers to the following questions quickly and accurately:

> How much business am I doing?
>
> What are my expenses, and which of them appear to be too high?
>
> What is my gross profit margin, and my net profit?
>
> How much am I collecting on my charge business?
>
> What is the condition of my working capital?
>
> How much cash do I have on hand and in the bank?
>
> How much do I owe my suppliers?
>
> What is my net worth—that is, what is the value of my ownership of the business?
>
> What are the trends in my receipts, expenses, profits and net worth?
>
> Is my financial position improving or growing worse?
>
> What is the percentage of return on my investment?
>
> How many cents out of each dollar of sales are net profits?

Broadly speaking, then, your records should include those related to inventory and purchasing, sales records, cash records, credit, employee records (legally required; be sure they're kept), records of fixtures and property (needed for depreciation allowances and insurance coverage), and the usual records used in double-entry bookkeeping, if that is your system.

Be sure to keep your personal bank account separate from your business account, into which all your daily receipts should be deposited. If you want to draw money for your own use, write a check on the store account made out to yourself. Set up a petty cash fund to make small purchases, making out the checks to petty cash, and be sure to make a record of every payment. Never make payments from the cash drawer. Also, it is imperative that you reconcile your bank account monthly. Bank errors or mistakes of your own doing can foul up your bank balance and cause unnecessary embarrassment.

All of the above will help you to keep one more kind of record—a budget. A budget will aid you in determining how much of a profit increase you can reasonably expect, and will tell you what sales you'll need to get your desired profit, what fixed expenses are going to be necessary to support the sales, what variable expenses are going to be incurred. In brief, your budget sets a goal and tells you what you have to do to reach it. Compare it with your actual operations from time to time, and if your records are effective, you'll be able to pinpoint discrepancies and correct them before it's too late. Whether you make the right decisions will depend on how much you can learn about management techniques in buying, pricing, selling, selecting and training personnel, and so on—in brief, all the things we've been talking about in this book. Experience will certainly help as you go along; the rest depends on your ability to accumulate information and learn from it.

18

Getting into Retailing with a Franchise

SINCE SO MANY PEOPLE ARE BECOMING instant retailers these days through the franchise approach, it could be helpful to give you a few plain facts about what is involved in the franchising game before you decide whether or not to take that route. There is a certain amount of confusion about franchising on the part of the public, but it's basically a simple operation. Only the specific applications are complicated.

A good definition of modern franchising has not yet been coined, so the word is misused and abused. An expert in the business whom I respect offers this definition: it is a system of distributing goods or services that combines the best features of a large chain operation and a completely independent small business. It isn't a business as such, but rather a way of carrying on a business—a mixed form of business organization.

Franchising is used in many ways, over a broad range of business activity. Everyone knows the most successful of these franchise operations—MacDonald's, H.&R. Block, AAMCO Transmissions, Holiday Inns, Snap-on Tools, Burger King, to name some outstanding ones that come quickly to mind. However it works, there are some elements that must always be present if the business is to be a true franchise and not simply a distributorship, or a licensed dealer, or a wholesaler. The basic requirements are the authorized use of a trademark and a long-term, ongoing relationship between the franchising company and the businessman who holds the franchise. Both must agree to abide by certain rules of business conduct designed to make the operation successful.

It's possible to divide franchising into three broad classes: franchises distributing a particular *product* under the manufacturer's name, like auto dealerships; *entire format* franchises, combining the use of a trade name and a method of doing business, like the fast food restaurants, motels, and business services; and those combining elements of both, such as soft drink bottlers. There are also convenience store franchises, specialized auto service centers, tax and business consultants, employment agencies, printing, tool, and even employee motivation franchises.

In recent years, franchising has become a major part of the American marketing system. There are about 900 franchising companies, with more than 400,000 franchised businesses. They account for about $158 billion or 27 percent of all retail sales in the United States. With services added, the total sales come to $177 billion.

Most of this total comes from traditional kinds of franchisers, familiar to us in different guises for the past 50 years. But there is a substantial growth segment in the industry, with emphasis on newer kinds of businesses. Nine out of every 10 franchising companies today are less than 20 years old, and in that time, these firms have spawned more than 200,000 franchised businesses. A quarter of all restaurant sales, for example, comes from franchised outlets. The system as a whole provides jobs for 3,300,000 people.

If you've been working hard accumulating some capital and have decided you're tired of working for someone else, you're a good candidate for a franchise operation. You'll have to be convinced you can make it on your own and be willing to take the risks involved. You could go into business for yourself in the traditional way, of course, as I've been advocating in this book, but before you make that decision you owe it to yourself to consider the advantages of going into a franchised business. There you'll be selling merchandise with instantly recognizable trademarks reflecting national reputations and you'll be dealing with companies that provide you with management expertise and sophisticated advertising. The Small Business Administration reminds us: "Without franchising, thousands of small businessmen would never have had the opportunity of owning their own businesses."

Franchising will give you the opportunity to compete with giant, vertically integrated corporations, and a good chance to avoid the 93 percent of retail business failures which are the result of inexperience and/or incompetence. If you come from a minority group or an otherwise less advantaged segment of the population, franchising can open the door to advancement. The number of minority-owned franchises increases steadily, and some companies have established formal programs to help people in this category.

Be careful to avoid the unscrupulous companies that call themselves franchisers but really aren't. Pyramid schemes, for example, where the so-called franchise is simply a license to lure in other victims, are not franchising, and neither are the phony rack-jobbing and vending machine frauds, or worthless distributorships. Legitimate franchisers are members of the International Franchise Association, which is pledged to a strict code of ethics and insists on full and accurate disclosure of all material information to potential franchisees before they commit themselves. The Association will send you a booklet titled "Investigate Before Investing," which explains how to look past promises and get the facts, how to check out products and management in a franchise company and how to obtain information on fees, start-up costs, and contract terms. It will even help you to evaluate yourself as a potential franchise retailer. Write to the International Franchise Association, 7315 Wisconsin Ave., Washington, D. C., 20014.

Evaluating the System

If you're interested in going into a franchise business, you will have to make two critical evaluations before you begin. It goes without saying that you'll investigate the company offering the franchise, but you'll have to analyze yourself as well. It's a point that people often overlook. Not everybody is qualified to run a franchise operation, for any number of reasons—experience, or lack of it, physical incapabilities, lack of education, learning disabilities, financial status, and ill-temperament.

In any self-examination, the first thing you should do is to set down what your interests and abilities really are, because they are often the best guide to what kind of franchise you should undertake. For example, if you're mechanically minded, you might well consider an auto repair franchise. Or if you're good with figures, you'd do better to look into a business service franchise, let's say, instead of a fast food outlet.

You will have to be mentally prepared for both hard work and financial risk. Ask yourself some hard questions:

> Am I good at managing others?
>
> Would I be reluctant to get my hands dirty in the business?
>
> Would operating a franchised business fit the image I have of myself, and the way I live?

Have I consulted with family, friends, and advisers that I trust and respect?

Experts in this field agree that temperament is critically important. Franchised businesses require their people to adhere to certain standards of quality and uniformity; this means you'll have to ask yourself how well you react to authority or restraints. If you've always been a lone wolf, or if originality and creativity are important to you, chances are you won't be comfortable in franchising.

Franchise Opportunities

Once you've made your self-evaluation and concluded that this is, in fact, the business path you want to follow, then it is time to look over franchise opportunities. This is a two-way street: the franchisers will be looking you over, too, because they have a large stake in the success of the people they franchise and they don't want to make mistakes.

In the booklet "Investigate Before Investing" (again, let me recommend it to you), the International Franchise Association advises potential franchisees to consider the product or service first, rather than the franchising company itself. Further, it ought to be a proven product, not something new and untried, and it must be applicable to your area—what good is an outdoor swimming pool franchise in a very cold climate where the summer season is only two months long? Ask yourself, too, what competition you will have to face, and whether there are any patents or trade secrets involved where your right to use them might be in question. Check on whether there are any government standards and regulations involved which you ought to know about.

With these questions answered, you can begin to look at individual franchisers. There are more than 900 of them, and there are directories that list them, notably the Franchise Opportunities Handbook, published by the United States Chamber of Commerce. Don't confine your exploration of any company to this single source. Get outside information, checking carefully the financial health and strength of the franchiser, its management structure and the source of its earnings. If it's a publicly held company, this data will be available in any library. If it is privately held, use the International Franchise Association's classified directory of members. You might also check with the regional Small Business Administration office, the Federal Trade Commission office and the Better Business Bureau. Credit reports can be obtained from firms like Dun & Bradstreet.

If you're completely new to the franchise business, find out how much training you can get from the franchiser. Some operate schools for new recruits, and others provide follow-up training and emergency assistance. It's a good thing to know just how much you can expect from the company. Many of them have field representatives who visit their franchisees, giving them tips and advice on merchandising methods, accounting practices, personnel policies, and so on. It's important to find out in advance what the company will do for you in terms of site selection, how much advertising support you can expect, and what policies and restrictions go along with the franchise.

The kit should contain a profit projection. If it doesn't, ask for one. That's a key point, obviously, since the prime object of going into business for yourself is to make money. But have the figures and assumptions checked by an accountant.

What To Expect

On the other side of the profit coin, of course, is the question of costs. Don't forget that the franchise business is like any other; you'll be expected to invest your own capital at the beginning. At that point you will need a lawyer to look over the franchise contract, and this is doubly important because no two contracts are alike. The lawyer will be able to explain franchise fees to you, continuing royalties, training costs, other fees, and start-up costs. You need to arrive at the start-up costs and have an estimate of continuing expenditures.

There are many other things in that franchise contract you'll want to know—such items as the right to sell or transfer ownership of your franchise, the right to renew, the provisions for termination of the contract, territorial rights, competition from other franchisers and company-owned units, and the extent of your obligation to purchase supplies and materials from the franchiser, or from franchiser-designated companies.

While you're going over the contract, you and your lawyer should watch for those flashing danger signs that indicate a shady operation. Be on your guard against franchises that promise big profits on small investments; demand that you act immediately without investigating; fail to identify their company officers or to provide other vital statistics, and use names that are similar to nationally known, reputable firms. One excellent way to check up on a franchiser is to talk to franchisees who are already working for the company. You should be doubly careful of a franchiser who is reluctant to identify all his franchisees.

You will get some protection in the several states that have adopted franchise disclosure laws designed to make full information available to potential investors. Regrettably, these laws sometimes confuse as much as they enlighten because the requirements of the states are very often different from each other, making matters particularly difficult for franchisers who are operating nationwide. Through the International Franchise Association's efforts, all nine of the states with disclosure laws now accept a uniform offering circular providing full information about a company.

Nevertheless, these statements have their limitations. "Investigate Before Investing" tells us: "You should not assume that the registration of a franchise or the preparation of a disclosure statement for use in your state means that the information in the statement is complete, accurate and free of excessive claims and misleading statements or that the administrative agency of your state has in any way approved the franchise. Independent verification of the information contained in a disclosure statement is essential if you are to do a thorough job of investigating before you invest."

Investing in a Franchise

Let's sum up, then, what you should do before you invest in a franchise. Here's a checklist:

> *Get professional assistance in evaluating financial claims and contracts.*
>
> *Determine the inherent salability of the product or service.*
>
> *Check the history and track record of the franchise company and its management.*
>
> *Find out if the company accepts and follows the International Franchise Association's code of ethics and ethical advertising code.*
>
> *Talk to other franchisees.*
>
> *Subject yourself to an honest self-analysis of your own capabilities, motivations and goals.*

If all this sounds difficult and complicated, remember that you would be well advised to do much the same thing if you were going to start out in any other kind of business. It may be well worth the effort, furthermore, because the skills and public acceptance of franchise companies combined with individual energy and resourcefulness have created a system accounting for nearly one-third of all retail sales in this country today.

As you weigh in your mind whether to go into franchising or not, it may be useful to sum up a few of the arguments for doing it in addition to those already stated. First, if you have limited experience, you'll be able to take advantage of a franchiser's experience and expertise. It will take a relatively small amount of capital for you to start—from $7,000 minimum to as much as $150,000 maximum, with most falling into the $10,000 category—and you'll have a ready-made financial and credit standing you might not have otherwise, along with a well-developed consumer image and good will as the result of proven products and services. There are also some other advantages:

> You will have the decided advantage of expertly designed facilities, layout, displays and fixtures.

> You will be the beneficiary of the buying power that comes only from chain operation.

> You will have an opportunity to get business training and continuing assistance from experienced management people in proven methods of doing business.

> You'll have the substantial help of national or regional promotion and publicity that might well take you a long time to achieve as an independent.

Those are the chief advantages, but as in any other kind of human activity, there are also disadvantages:

> A sticking point with many people will be the fact that they will have to submit to imposed standardized operations. The franchiser advertisements claim that you'll be your own boss, and in a sense you will be, but you will definitely not have the freedom to make decisions in many areas.

> You will have to share profits with the franchiser.

> You won't have the freedom to meet local competition because you won't have the flexibility of making your own decisions.

> There is the danger that contracts will be slanted to the franchiser's advantage.

> Be prepared for what may seem like an inordinate amount of time to prepare reports required by the franchiser, and for the times when you may have to share the burden of his faults if the chain comes into public disfavor for any reason.

Where To Look

After weighing the pros and cons, one question remains: Where do you look for franchise opportunities? The classified sections of daily newspapers, under "Business Opportunities," are a good source. If only a box number is listed, this usually means the franchiser is making a preliminary screening to eliminate "shoppers" from "buyers." Trade publications are another good source (franchisers advertise in those related to their business), and so are franchising publications, for example, *National Franchise Reports*, published by Continental Reports, Denver, Colorado. There are frequent franchiser exhibitions in major cities which give you an opportunity to meet company representatives and compare offers. Be wary of anyone who wants to sign a contract on the spot. Finally, there are franchise marketing agencies and franchise consultants who will help prospective investors to find a profitable business. They also provide information on particular companies and their franchisees. This assistance will cost you a little extra money, but it may be worth it.

19

The Automatic Vending Business

IF YOU WANT TO BE YOUR OWN BOSS without going into franchising, you should consider the automatic vending business, a branch of retailing that has been growing with startling rapidity since the end of World War II. It's easy to see why this is so if you look around and observe the number of coin-operated devices into which millions of Americans deposit their small change every day. The machines will sell you everything from candy bars to full lunches, paper towels to clean laundries, foot massages to comb-and-tonic hair treatments, besides photographs, copies of birth certificates, newspapers, books, parking spaces, stamps—the list goes on and on. In 1976, there were more than 4 million vending machines in the United States selling more than $4 billion worth of goods and services annually.

Looks promising, doesn't it? But as with any other kind of retailing, nobody should go into the vending machine business without analyzing it and himself first. This chapter will give you some guidelines.

Venders dispense products consumed or used on the spot, or provide services such as scales, photos, shoeshines and laundry and dry-cleaning. Vending has become a great deal more complicated than it used to be, and much more varied. It has followed the pattern of other businesses in becoming increasingly specialized. Some operators carry only one kind of business—candy, cigarettes, milk, ice cream, coffee, stamps. About 18 percent of those in the business specialize in one kind of machine, while 14 percent offer only two different lines. The majority, however, still handle four or more kinds of products.

Bulk venders, as they are called—that is, those selling such items as stamps, cosmetics, grooming aids, school supply items and gum balls—usually don't add other items, because the locations of their machines don't lend themselves to diversification and also because the machines themselves are less expensive than other, more complicated kinds, and operators don't want to risk additional capital. For anyone but a bulk vender, however, it's good economic sense to add more lines. Many companies offer several different machines that vend coffee, soft drinks, juices, milk, ice cream, candy, gum, cigarettes, canned soup, hot and cold sandwiches, salads, pastry, desserts, cookies and crackers— even complete hot entrees or casseroles.

There's a considerable difference between full-line vending and smaller operations. For the former, a great new market has been created by shorter lunch hours, on-the-job eating and drinking and the rising cost of conventional food services. All this has led to more full-line vending. Small operators who go into this area of the business must be prepared to expand quickly, to add employees, learn new skills, and raise more capital. The problem is that they are going to be in competition with conventional food-service contractors and their vending departments. That makes it a crowded and highly competitive field—no place for amateurs.

Tasks and Pitfalls

Fortunately for the beginner, most vending machines are in small offices or plants, theatres, restaurants, cocktail lounges, transportation terminals, service stations, motels and similar locations. These places usually have only one or two machines, and small operators are able to compete on much better terms with the larger companies. They can turn a profit on smaller volume, and since there are so many locations of this kind still to be served, the opportunities to expand and grow are numerous.

Wherever you operate a vending business, your tasks and problems will involve much the same kind of work. You'll be buying machines, placing them on location, repairing and changing them as needed, refilling and servicing them at regular intervals, and collecting, counting and depositing the coins. Besides all that, you will have to maintain headquarters where you can keep your merchandise, supplies and parts along with facilities for repairs, coin counting, sanitation and bookkeeping.

You will need such basic equipment as a station wagon or truck to take you on the rounds of your machines, and that will be true no matter how small the business. The organization is much like that of a milk or a dry-cleaning route. In small towns, there will be only one route. In cities, it is most effective to limit yourself to one section at the beginning; then lay out the business along several routes as you expand, maintaining an efficient travel pattern. Routes don't usually go beyond a 30- or 50-mile radius. Even the large operator who has routes in several cities has to have a headquarters in each one. It's basically a local operation.

To understand the nature of the vending machine business, it's necessary to know that it exists because these machines are able to sell products and services at times and in places where other kinds of retailing can't do as well and when around-the-clock sales over the counter aren't profitable (which would be most of the time). Vending machines cater to impulse buyers, and so their sales are extra sales—made because the machine is handy. That tells you why the location is so important. Successful vendors are guided by both experience and intuition when they're spotting locations. They know that their average volume of sales per machine is going to be low, and that profit per machine is going to be small. The trick is to get enough volume per machine, and in the total operation, to earn profits.

It isn't as easy to get into the vending machine business as it may seem. You will first have to find potentially profitable locations and get the owner to let you install machines, in return for monthly commissions based on sales. Then you have to be a merchandiser, just as you would in any other business, and decide on what brands you're going to stock, how to rotate products, how to place the machine—these among many other skills. Vending may be called automatic merchandising, but it's only the machines that are automatic; the business operation itself takes skill, intelligence and hard work.

The machines have to be chosen according to model and size in relation to the planned location, and you have to know where to buy them. Consult the U.S. Chamber of Commerce booklet referred to in the preceding chapter. You will also have to find out what city and state licensing regulations apply. Then there's the usual necessity of installing bookkeeping and other kinds of record keeping.

Maybe it still sounds simple to you. All that has to be done is to get the machines, install and stock them, collect, and watch the money roll in. But there are bear traps all over the place—one that kills off many beginners is poor equipment. When a machine is out of order, it isn't earning a penny, and in the vending business every penny counts. You lose customers, too, with a machine that doesn't work. There's also a certain amount of fraud among vending machine promotions. Dishonest dealers will sell you faulty machines for a high price, and then leave town. Never deal with anyone but reputable machine manufacturers. It's always a good idea to compare what's offered by different companies before you decide.

Obsolescence is another problem in the business. When a manufacturer starts refining his product, or takes a new approach, it may mean problems for small operators. If you had been vending instant coffee when the fresh-brew coffee people came along, for instance, you would have had to upgrade your operation or lose your locations. New machines are always a threat to your investment in old equipment.

Perhaps the most important thing to watch out for as you enter the vending business is to be sure your commissions are sound. Not every new location necessarily means good business. Accurate record keeping will weed out the bad ones. Keep a record of the performance of every machine, evaluate sales against costs, and allow yourself a proper profit margin. What is proper will be conditioned by the size of the commission you pay the location owner; it is usually a percentage of gross sales. If you think you have to pay commissions that are too large in order to get a location—to "buy" new business, so to speak—you had better be prepared to cut corners on service and the quality of the product to make up for the loss. Obviously, that isn't good business. You'll not only be eating into your profits soon, but you'll be less able to build up a reserve in case you need to expand.

There are two other pitfalls worth mentioning. One is the vandalism and burglary problem, particularly with outdoor locations. Thieves know where supervision is impossible, which makes their job easier, and vandals can and will damage your equipment in their mindless way. Locks and burglar alarms help, but a better means of prevention is to choose locations where these risks are minimized. The other problem is even worse in a way—slugs. A slug delivers as much merchandise as if it had been a real coin, but without the income. You'll be lucky if it's a foreign coin. There are laws against slugs, but trapping those who use them is not foremost on the list of police priorities, and even if it were, it wouldn't be easy. There's not much you can do about it, except to abandon a location where the use of slugs threatens to wipe out your profit.

If that's necessary, cheer up. A recent list of possible locations in a typical city showed more than 70 different kinds of locations, from airports to zoos, and it was a relatively short list. As in other businesses ingenuity and perseverance are rewarded in the vending business.

Retailing in the Years Ahead

20

Opportunities—Today and Tomorrow

OVER THE PAST FEW YEARS, stores displaying *Going Out of Business* signs have become familiar sights. The bankruptcy of the W. T. Grant variety store chain and the closing of many A&P supermarkets left many thousands of units of real estate on the market. Numerous storefronts in once-thriving central business districts carry FOR RENT signs rather than FOR SALE signs; parking lots for many freestanding units now play host to weeds rather than cars; shoppers stroll by boarded-up stores in once totally-leased shopping centers. And the situation is not limited to previously occupied units; ground-floor space in new downtown skyscrapers hopelessly await first tenants while a fair number of spanking new malls open their doors with a 25 percent vacancy rate.

In light of all these facts, it's clear that during the next several years, retailers and landlords will have to use their imaginations to find some solutions. However, to the credit of the retail community, much progress has been made. In late 1976, the International Council of Shopping Centers revealed that almost 80 percent of the W. T. Grant stores were re-occupied. Similarly, *Chain Store Age Executive* reported in January 1977 that roughly 85 percent of the shuttered A&P super-markets were rented to independent grocers, as well as retailers of a totally different calling. Drug chains and fabric outlets, for instance, have found ex-supermarkets in the 10,000 square foot class to be excellent and inexpensive vehicles for expansion. Similarly, specialized mass merchandisers, such as toy merchandisers and home improvement and catalog operators, have made good use of former discount stores.

Still, supply exceeds demand and landlords must realize that the failures and reorganizations of the past few years have produced a retail industry which is more interested in showing its stockholders a solid bottom line rather than a record number of openings.

What the Landlord Can Do

Here's where the *creativity* must emerge. A number of frustrated property owners have simply decided that no worthwhile retailer would be interested in their space and have converted the premises into skating rinks, offices, warehouses, annexes, etc. This may be fine in the case of a freestanding building, but when conversion of retailing space takes place in a shopping center or central business district, it may be no better for the remaining tenants than leaving the space vacant. In the long run, it is usually in the landlord's best interest to fill that space with a retail establishment.

In the early 1970s, when discount stores were being abandoned by the hundreds, landlords found themselves without a large number of legitimate space-takers. One popular method used to fill these spaces was the creation of a flea market or part-time shopping center on the premises, operated by the landlord or others. However, unless these units were professionally run, the operations usually failed.

Other attempts at improvisation with professional guidance can produce more effective use of vacant space. For example, a landlord of a new skyscraper faced with a vacant 5000 square-foot ground-floor store should consider opening his own operation in the space—and with assistance from retail professionals, feature branded men's and women's sportswear. Employees of tenants in the building could be given discount cards to purchase goods in the store well below prices in conventional department stores.

What the Retailer Can Do—Mini Department Stores

Creativity need not only be at the whim of the landlord. Retailers can develop new ventures, especially with smaller spaces in the 10,000 square-foot range. In 1976 a major American corporation created a number of mini-department stores in 10,000 square-foot former super-markets in the Southwest. Merchandise is limited to profitable and fast-moving family sportswear, jewelry, cosmetics, accessories, records, small appliances and housewares. Items are strictly brand names and are displayed in a setting comparable to the main floor of any conven-tional department store. Since opening the four Thomas & Hart stores in 1976, Southland plans to add two more in 1977.

With the advent of the mini-department store developed along this formula, equally intriguing are the new directions underway in the large department store business. Most significantly, the old axiom of catering to all customers' needs is going by the wayside. The result is that department stores are gearing to a fashion-oriented image and limiting their mixes to a particular price range. In an age of specializa-tion, retailing's general practitioners are being forced to specialize to a degree, and the reason is simply survival.

Department stores can no longer afford to carry large inventories of every product under the sun. Moreover, with store sizes shrinking, such practices are becoming physically impossible—nobody builds stores like Macy's Herald Square anymore. In trying to solve the dilemma of competition in price and selection for speciality items such as appliances and designer apparel lines, department stores have turned to the alternatives of stocking limited quantities and offering better selections in a more limited number of lines. In doing so, the stores have chosen to put their money in fashion merchandise and to shrink the less profitable hard lines departments. To compete with spe-ciality stores, the department stores are placing even more emphasis on shop areas—assigned to anything from denims to designer casuals.

This fashion focus will continue to influence store design and con-struction. Because of the volatile nature of fashion, store design must be able to readily adapt to changing merchandise. As such, the trend to flexible walls and fixturing will continue, as well as the devoting of more time and money to marketing research, studies of buying habits, demographics, etc.

Employee Stores

The employee store is a new version of something very old—years ago it was called a company store and was a symbol of worker exploitation by managements which controlled nearly every aspect of their employees' lives. Since the stores were usually located in isolated com-munities, the workers had no choice but to buy everything they needed at the company store where high prices and extended credit further obligated the employee to the employer.

Today the employee store has no resemblance to the old model. Physically, it is generally an area from 1000 to 2000 square feet on the premises of a large corporation and is operated for the benefit of the employees, who have many other choices if they care to make them. Many banks in the New York metropolitan area, for example, have created such stores for their employees, as have most of the large corporations outside the city in the fast-growing industrial parks. While these stores are no longer power instruments for management, they still leave much to be desired.

The typical employee store—General Electric's and Philip Morris's are two that come readily to mind—sell mostly cigarettes, candy, newspapers, cookies and in the case of General Electric, some of the company's own appliances and radios. There is an effort to make available some major appliances at reasonable prices, rather than simply wholesale. But all these stores fall far short of their possibilities, in my opinion. The problem with most employee stores we've seen is that they're not professionally run: merchandise mix, buying, presentation, controls and personnel are inadequate. The result is that the units operate at a loss and are not even catering to the workers' desires.

I believe the minimum size for an employee store on the premises should be at least 2000 square feet. The classifications of items that belong in such a store include health and beauty aids, small appliances, radios, portable television sets, cassette players, men's and ladies' apparel, a complete housewares department, Timex watches, and calculators. If you don't see these classifications in an employee store, it doesn't have much reason for existing.

Fortunately, some companies are beginning to give their employee stores the same kind of scrutiny as they would apply to any benefit program that was proving a failure. For instance, with the help of professional consultants, one major bank in New York revamped its two units in 1976. Sales subsequently soared from $200 per square foot to $300-$400, and deficits were erased. It's our feeling that other corporations will seek to follow a similar course in the years ahead. What effect employee stores will have on the competitive retail situation outside the companies remains to be seen. I believe the impact will be slight, but we'll have to wait to find out.

Savings Bank Stores

Still another possible new development in retailing in the next few years will be a retail store organized by and identified with a savings bank. Since the early 1970s, savings banks have been giving away "free gifts" in return for deposits of various sizes from new customers. For example, a new customer depositing $500 may receive a toaster. The larger the amount deposited, the more valuable the gift.

To give you an idea of how successful this idea of premiums has been, consider the case of the Bowery Savings Bank when it opened a new branch in New York City in 1976. In a 30-day period, the total amount of new deposits was $60 million. The cost of the items the bank gave away to attract the deposits amounted to about $1 million at cost. For the bank this was obviously a resounding success: the branch showed profit from the opening day.

However, this highly successful plan, used by so many banks, is not without flaws. The chief problem is that after one year, the minimum contract time for a deposit, the customer may remove his money and deposit it in another bank which has just announced the opening of a branch. The depositors, in effect, are playing musical chairs with their deposits. A sufficient number of people play this game to worry the banks, but not enough, apparently, to impair their scheme substantially.

The retail concept which I believe will diminish this problem for the banks would be the establishment of a store to carry a broad line of desirable, nationally advertised merchandise. The bank would issue membership cards to all its depositors who keep an amount above a certain figure—let's say $250. Possession of the card would entitle the depositor to buy any of the merchandise in the store at close to wholesale prices, about 10 percent over cost. Thus the merchandise would be sold at a very reasonable figure and the 10 percent margin would cover the overhead of the store, so that it would be self-supporting and not an extra expense for the bank.

I don't argue that this plan would end the game of musical chairs, but it would certainly lessen the number of people who make total withdrawals and thus help the bank retain more of its new depositors.

I have discussed this idea with the executives of Channel 13, the public television station in New York, as a possible means of income for the station and to supplement its membership drives. I have suggested that they create a members-only store, either on or off their premises, with membership limited to their employees and anyone making a donation to the station at a certain monetary level. Such a store, I believe, would be a major help to public broadcasting, which must look for money anywhere it can be found. For employees, it would be an example of altruism, and for the public, it would be an incentive to subscribe. While neither Channel 13 nor any other public broadcaster has yet to try this idea, I think it is safe to predict that many of them will in the near future.

Mini-Employee Stores

One of the most fascinating developments currently taking place in the retail community is the increasing use of gasoline stations—or rather their misuse—as merchandise outlets. Faced with rising costs, like every other business, thousands of stations are converting to self-service operations or closing down altogether. Today there is a movement toward making the former bay areas, where cars were serviced, into something productive. Many kinds of experimental retail outlets are being tried—bicycle stores, small superettes, gift shops, and a variety of others—but with little success. I believe a better solution exists for these bay areas (between 500 and 1500 square feet) which would offer new and lucrative opportunities.

One possibility would be for the oil company which owns the station to establish something like a mini-employee store, that is, a comparatively small space stocked with such reliables as health and beauty aids, housewares, automotive goods, hardware, and depending on the space, electronics. The most exciting possibility, however, for this type of outlet would be in selling home entertainment equipment. It would be a potential gold mine to stock these stores with such items as the new video discs when they emerge at mass prices, records, tapes, cassettes, radios, cassette players, tape recorders, packaged stereo systems, and portable television sets. It's easy to visualize these home entertainment centers stretching from coast to coast under the sign of Texaco, Citgo, Mobil, or any one of the other giants. The advertising advantages alone from such an arrangement are tremendous. These companies have mailing systems running into millions of names, so that with every credit mailing they could include advertising for the merchandise in these centers. I'm convinced that this would be a remarkable opportunity for the oil companies to get into the entertainment business and increase their revenues.

While the kind of stores I've just described would be my first choice, I have another idea for these empty bay areas. The companies ought to make a study of what might result from turning them into insurance offices. The advantages are obvious. Insurance is big business, too, and the merger of interests would be a natural one. Each would advertise the other across the country. It's an idea worth at least a feasibility study. All these possibilities, just mentioned, are intended for corporate giants, however, not individual entrepreneurs.

A Retailing Boost—The Video Disc

Perhaps I'd better say something more about this video disc I've been referring to, particularly since it represents a future multi-billion dollar business in this country.

The video-audio disc looks like an ordinary phonograph record except that it has three holes in the center instead of the customary one. Two major corporations are involved competitively in developing and marketing it, RCA and the international consortium known as MCA-Phillips. The disc is seen and heard through a player connected to your television set. Since it is removed from the vagaries of antenna transmission, the picture is perfect, comparable to the far more expensive video tape systems.

As was the case with early color television, the RCA and Phillips systems are not compatible. Experts believe MCA-Phillips has more sophisticated technology and will eventually emerge as the winner, but that remains to be proved. I believe both will prevail, in much the same way that RCA's 45 rpm records and CBS's 33⅓ long-playing records learned to live together, even though the 45's quickly came to occupy a distinctly secondary position.

Whether there are one or two systems is unimportant, however. We're interested only in the potential sales of video discs and players of whatever make. If you look upon the discs as home movies, it is easy to see why they will have a tremendous impact on the nation's entertainment habits. As with the introduction of any new technology, older technologies will feel the competition in varying degrees—the publishing business, commercial television, and at least the second-run movie houses. Not that they will disappear; book publishing, after all, has survived every competitor for the attention of readers since the introduction of the bicycle, and keeps right on growing.

Video discs and players are scheduled for commercial debut in 1977. Initial drawbacks have been anticipated, and titles will be limited until people discover their potential uses. Not only will your old favorite movies of Gable and Bogart be available, but all the current films as well. And that's only the beginning. The discs will be a superb educational medium, offering such things as "How To Repair Your Electric Wiring," "How To Repair the Plumbing," "How To Improve Your Golf Game" (or tennis, or any other sport), and an expanding list of similar home instruction items. Children will have a large choice of visual entertainment which television now virtually denies them. The possibilities of the new medium, clearly, are almost unlimited.

As the video disc makes its debut, retailers will have an opportunity to add a video disc library to their stock, with the option of renting the discs or selling them outright. The product requires little space—a six-foot wall behind a counter would be sufficient to carry a library of all the best sellers. Profits would depend upon the volume, which should, considering the potential, be great. Also, it's quite possible to retail video discs and players from the home, at least in some locations. We can look for new producers coming out of the ranks of corporations such as the food chains (individually or as a consortium), the major

food franchisers (MacDonald's, Burger King and others), the big air-
lines, real estate interests, cigarette and can companies, and oil companies. The corporations won't have it all to themselves. As I've
attempted to make clear, there are also possibilities for imaginative
and ambitious individuals. Some of these small investors will become
the success stores of the future—and I hope there will be many of
them.

Industrial Parks

Still another area of new retail development is occurring in the industrial parks, a phenomenon of the past few years. I'm thinking about a
particular park in New Jersey, facing New York across the Hudson
River. It is a huge complex of buildings built by the owners of Hartz
Mountain Pet Products. Many firms are quartered there, some having
their home offices and distribution centers in the same building. Most,
in fact, are in that category, although in many the distribution may be
only for that part of the country. Panasonic and many nationally
advertised apparel manufacturers are tenants, as well as companies
like Mikasa, importers and manufacturers of fine and casual dinner-
ware.

On weekends many of these distribution centers in the park are
open to the general public, and the amount of traffic and business generated from them is incredible. The crush is often so great that private
traffic police have to be employed to handle the surge of vehicles and
people coming to make what are usually substantial purchases. Presumably, this kind of thing is happening in other industrial parks all
over the country, and there are hundreds, perhaps thousands, of them.
This is certainly a business which the retail community ought to
examine, with an interested eye toward the future. It seems to me a
practical way for the major manufacturers to raise immediate cash.

Let's use Mikasa as an example, assuming they participate in this
kind of selling. When they sell their product to department stores they
will generally wait about 50 to 60 days before they get paid. Imagine
how desirable it would be for them to sell the merchandise and be paid
immediately. Since they're not selling their products at the same low
price they sell to department stores, they get a double benefit—that is,
they're making a higher profit on each sale and getting paid
immediately in hard cash.

Another interesting aspect of this situation is that when all these
firms signed leases to come into the industrial parks, no consideration was
given by either the companies or the real estate developers of the park
to the possible growth of such a substantial retail business. By this

time the developers must be aware of what is taking place, and no doubt as new firms rent space in the industrial parks, they will insert a percentage clause covering retail sales.

Factory Outlet Stores

Another interesting wrinkle in the fabric of American retailing is the factory store. Nothing is new or startling about that kind of selling, of course; it had its origins in the nineteenth century, if not earlier. But in the past few years, this kind of business has been proliferating rapidly. In fact, when new factories are constructed provisions are often made for such a store. Again, this is hardly a new development, but lately it has been spreading in a much more organized way than in the past.

For example, in Western Pennsylvania there are now organized bus tours that take potential customers from highly populated urban areas to factories where they are invited to buy any merchandise that happens to be on hand. Do the customers save money? Possibly, even probably. But do they buy at true wholesale prices? Certainly not. For the most part, these customers are probably exposed to some older merchandise that didn't sell, along with some new merchandise. But this kind of selling does take a bite out of the conventional retail community's profits. It isn't a serious bite, and there is not much possibility that it will be, but it exists and it is growing.

The success of this concept is borne out in its proliferation. Iris Ellis, author of a book on such establishments, says that there were 8,000 outlets in the United States in 1976, contrasted with 1,000 in 1971.

A more serious aspect of this kind of retail selling by manufacturers is found in the giant multifirm manufacturing organizations which have developed over a period of time retail arms of some size and importance. In the early 1970s, I had a meeting with three executives of Kayser-Roth about the directions they were taking in retailing their own product. They told me they had created the office of vice-president for retail sales, and that they possessed well-planned blueprints for their future in this field.

In large residential areas on the West Coast, these executives said, they had been opening factory stores identified with the parent company and selling their specific products. I asked them to what extent these stores would impair their sales, specifically their bathing suits, on the West Coast or in other areas where they were opening outlets. They told me there was no effect whatsoever on sales, and I found it amazing that the big retail department stores and chains would not have started to boycott those products.

Kayser-Roth was also operating a chain of small stores throughout the Southeast, selling their line of men's socks and women's pantyhose. Far from being hurt by the factory stores, they said, the chain was showing very satisfactory profits and they were extremely pleased. In fact, this noted apparel manufacturer's experience is not unique, but rather the norm for the industry. It's a general practice for such manufacturers to operate retail facilities "for the public" at their factories, warehouses or showrooms. I remember an executive of Manhattan Industries boasting to me of $150,000 promotion at their warehouse during a single weekend.

Revitalizing Real Estate

While some people may think the idea is an odd one, I'm convinced that another development in the retail business will be its involvement with real estate interests. Although these interests have extensive problems, particularly in urban areas, there is still the possibility of productive use of space in any area.

Walking around New York, for instance, a nonprofessional could not help being amazed by the large number of FOR RENT signs on retail stores, while office space has gone begging all over Manhattan in both old and new buildings. The spectacle of newly constructed office buildings standing empty, or nearly empty, is a startling thing to see. New York may be the hardest hit of the big cities, but it has no monopoly on the real estate problem. It is growing and there is no reason to believe it is going to get better before it gets much worse.

In 1976, I met with agents of the Metropolitan Life Insurance Company, a large holder of real estate in New York City, who agreed that a great deal of space was available which they were nearly desperate to fill. They asked me, in association with Penfield Retail Services, my New York management and consulting firm, to come in with plans and specifications, particularly for a space on Fifth Avenue between Forty-third and Forty-fourth Streets. The space was formerly a restaurant, of about 3000 square feet on the street level and 12,000 square feet on the lower level. We did as requested—I suggested that the owners design a junior department store on both levels and also supplied a cash flow chart and profit and loss statement.

We took a realistic point of view, bringing to bear our experience as retailers in New York for 30 years. The agent would have been happy to rent the lower level for $75,000 per year, but we planned a rental of more than double that amount, $175,000 per year, if the

agent or the owner would consider going into the retail business. We
pointed out that even if they merely broke even, they would still have
established a rental income of $175,000 on a vacant area for which
they had hoped to get only $75,000.

To our great disappointment, Metropolitan Life turned us down,
pleading that they didn't want to go into the retail business. If the offer
had been accepted, it would have meant the inauguration of a new
method for real estate people to make a good part of their non-produc-
tive space productive through a retail outlet.

Discount Stores

Many of the discounters who followed in the footsteps of E. J. Korvette
simply did not succeed. The real estate units these failures left behind
are, in most cases, poorly designed, drab inside and out, and too big for
their original purpose—all part of the reason for their demise.

The basic idea behind a discount store is to make available recognizable merchandise at low prices, but most of the so-called discounters
either never recognized that simple fact, or if they did, lost sight of it
as they continued to plunge into ruin. It is a fact that units of 100,000
and 140,000 square feet are simply impractical for a discount operation. Today, stores such as E. J. Korvette, Alexander's and May's can
no longer be considered discount stores—anyone who examines their
markup and their increased cost of doing business will realize that they
are not far behind the conventional department stores in these
respects.

A brilliant exception to what befell most of the discount stores is
the K-Mart chain, an offspring of the S. S. Kresge variety store organization. This new retail operation first appeared in Detroit in the 1960s
at a time when the Kresge people realized that the variety chain as it
then existed was going nowhere. For one thing, these variety stores
lacked merchandise charisma. Their locations were usually suspect; too
many were in the inner cities and the kind of merchandise sold didn't
generate enough customer interest and traffic.

Recognizing this situation, the extremely able Kresge executives in
Detroit determined to take their stores and mold them into viable,
attractive, exciting "discount" operations. Because of their superior
intelligence, organization, and understanding of the meaning of merchandising and redistribution, they emerged with a splendid example
of what a low-price, mass-merchandising operation should be.

On the present retail scene, the K-Marts dominate the low-price,
mass-merchandising field in which a huge part of the population does
its shopping. But when we examine heavily populated areas it appears

the K-Mart stores are not located where the major centers of population are, but rather they ring them, so to speak, because it is very difficult to find substantial pieces of property in major residential areas. However, it is in just these heavily populated areas that we find the empty supermarkets I've been mentioning, with their parking accommodations for anywhere from 50 to 100 cars. These vacant buildings are, in my opinion, excellent locations for discounting operations today. As I said, discounting today encompasses a bit more than it did 30 years ago when I started E.J. Korvette, meaning that in addition to offering the customer recognizable merchandise at low prices, the atmosphere and surroundings must be designed to add convenience and ease to one-stop shopping.

Perhaps the following list will offer some successful insights into setting up a discounting operation in tune with the times:

> COSMETICS—carry the famous brands but in each classification, carry only the best. If Max Factor and Revlon represent, let's say, 70 percent of all the cosmetic business in the United States, it ought to be enough to carry these two brands.

> JEWELRY—Timex should represent the bulk of your business in watches, but also carry the best-selling Seiko and Texas Instruments watches at higher prices. Also in this department include calculators from Texas Instruments and Rockwell, as well as the lower-priced models from Cascio and Sharp, in addition to the usual assortment of men's and ladies' jewelry.

> SMALL APPLIANCES—begin with clocks—digital, bedroom, kitchen—all primarily from General Electric. Also in this department include the best-selling brands of small appliances for hair care; other appliances such as steam irons, travel irons, toaster ovens, blenders, food mixers, electric hand mixers and possibly even Hoover vacuum cleaners should be carried.

> RADIOS—General Electric and Sony radio models should dominate the line; also include cassette players, tape recorders, packaged stereo sets, portable television sets and CB radios.

> POWER TOOLS—use the Black and Decker and Rockwell lines.

> MAJOR APPLIANCES—remember in a store such as this, the hard goods will have to be highly competitive. The goal would be a markup of at least 20 percent, and possibly

22 percent as a maintained figure on all well-known brands. Provide a good service and returns policy and familiarize the customer with these accommodations.

HOUSEWARES—include all the gadgetry and appurtenances vital to the refrigerator and the stove. Include also sets of Corelle, the individual pieces and the sets of Corningware, Farberware pots and pans and appliances, as well as Revereware, Wearever and any other significant cookingware that proves to be appropriate. This department should represent your highest markup.

RECORDS—this can be one of the most profitable departments in a store—in an area of about 1500 square feet it is quite possible that a good record department will sell anywhere from a quarter- to a half-million dollars annually.

READY-TO-WEAR LINES—in men's, ladies' and children's sportswear—using brands such as Wrangler, Levi, Farrah or Haggar, these lines represent, in my opinion, the kind of merchandise that is least prone to markdowns and which is also consistent with a good turnover. The ready-to-wear lines can also be mixed and matched with coordinating sportswear, especially sports shirts which outsell dress shirts at least two to one.

MEN'S FURNISHINGS—such as dress shirts, underwear, ties, belts—all should be brand-named and fine quality. The store's size would restrict you to carrying only the best sellers and to consider selling merchandise exempt from markdown.

When you've done your homework on this kind of operation and have worked out cash flows for such a store, prepared profit and loss statements, even at the most conservative figures, the bottom line comes out a success. In my opinion, and in that of many people with whom I've discussed these plans, this kind of store will be an important retail development in the years to come.

Team Stores

Of all the corporations that are, or may be, turning to retailing, the most surprising newcomers to the retail business are professional sports organizations, such as basketball, football, hockey and baseball.

Individual teams such as the New Orleans Jazz, the Buffalo Braves and the Detroit Pistons in basketball; the Baltimore Orioles, Minnesota Twins and Chicago White Sox in baseball; the New York (now in New Jersey) Giants in football; and the Philadelphia Flyers and Buffalo Sabres in hockey have already inquired into the possibility of setting up stores.

Club owners are looking into the retail possibilities of modest-sized sportswear and sporting goods stores as profitable year-round businesses. Another avenue is to use the club name for product endorsements and as a stimulus to ticket sales within the stores. When parents take their young children to the team stores to buy helmets or gloves, they will be able to pick up a tennis racket or a package of golf balls as well as tickets to the team's games.

Club product endorsements have already broken ground in New York. Shoppers can buy "New York Yankees" frankfurters in supermarkets, and I'm sure that manufacturers of elite brand-name luggage would be interested in national advertising with some of the teams. I have no doubt that meetings of club public relations personnel with sales promotion executives from retail ventures would produce a great many other profitable ideas. Sports executives are becoming increasingly aware that they must maximize the profitability of their franchises by making full use of whatever charisma their team name offers.

While at first glance it would appear that sporting goods and leisure wear are likely to comprise the stock of these sports stores, the planning I visualize is more ambitious. I'm thinking of a sporting goods store that would encompass, besides the obvious, jewelry, cosmetics, housewares, records, photography equipment, an electronic shop and a department featuring fine luggage, small leather goods and attaché cases. About 40,000 square feet would be a proper size for such a stock mix. All the merchandise would be elite brands, presented in a setting emphasizing celebrated sports figures. Such a retail establishment, in my opinion, would be a certain moneymaker, a prime stimulation for ticket sales and an ideal place to capitalize on club endorsements.

The "professionalizing" of employee stores, the growth of factory outlets, the specialization of department stores, the entry of landlords into retailing, the creation of mini-department stores, are all developments which will alter the face of retailing somewhat over the next few years. These will also offer a challenge to the smaller businessman. But change is not unique to the retail business—because of its closeness to the ultimate consumers, it must adapt to their needs more quickly than any other industry. Retailing simply cannot survive by standing still.

21

A Few Thoughts
about What It All Means

PEOPLE WHO WRITE ABOUT THEIR LIVES customarily save the last chapter
for a summing up of their philosophies and an attempt to assess their
life and works. In my own case, I have tried to tell the story of the
E.J. Korvette enterprises, created with a great deal of hard work, some
luck and more than a little innovation. I have emphasized that people
who want to go into retailing should not emulate me but try to create a
way of life for themselves that they will find fascinating and reward-
ing. I don't guarantee success, but I hope I've pointed out some of the
pathways to success and warned of the danger signs of failure.

My life in retailing has been an exciting one and continues to be
so. Now that the E. J. Korvette phase of it has ended, I find myself
going on in other directions, and in so doing I've been more and more
interested in observing what successful businessmen do with their
money, besides increase it. I have found that some are philan-
thropists—not only in the conventional sense, but also in the aesthetic.
Throughout the United States a kind of cultural renaissance has been
going on for some time as businessmen have been persuaded to turn
more of their money to the arts—not only to save existing institutions,
but also to help establish new ones. Books and magazine articles have
been written about "the new Medici," as they are sometimes called,
whose creative philanthropy has meant so much to music, art, ballet
and other aspects of our culture.

My father, if you'll recall, loved the arts and wanted me to spend more time with the arts at the beginning of my career. I refused and probably disappointed him, not because I didn't like music, the theatre, museums, libraries and all the rest, but because I was young and ambitious, frustrated by the years I had spent in the service and anxious to get into the retailing game and win it. My father, I thought, could afford to spend his time in the arts; he had already made his career.

As I grew older, however, my childhood love of the arts made me more and more appreciative of what was available to me in my home town, New York City. As a member of the business community, I was also increasingly aware of how much its leaders had contributed to make that cultural life possible. However some people might feel about the Rockefeller family politically, it is undeniable that their philanthropy has played a major role in the existence of the city's major art museums and Lincoln Center. The same could be said of other families across the country, entrepreneurs whose methods in accumulating wealth might be highly debatable but whose contributions to cultural institutions could only be called exemplary. Museums and libraries in many cities are monuments to the lives and fortunes of men who were generally disliked by many in their lifetimes.

The Metropolitan Museum of Art in New York City has been one of the treasures of my life. Whenever I could break away from business, which I'll admit was not very often, I would go there to follow my childhood practice of joining the lecture audiences. I remember with pleasure those afternoons when I walked from room to room with the teacher, beginning with Quatrocento art and ending with the Impressionists. Now I'm aware that J. P. Morgan and B. Altman money, particularly, had made those afternoons possible for me and so many others.

I have always thought of that other treasure, the Frick Collection, as having some of the finest paintings in one of the most beautiful settings in the world. Those paintings have become old friends through the years. As for the Frick mansion itself, I would love to move into it tomorrow. Henry Clay Frick, like J. P. Morgan, built his fortune by methods that could hardly be admired, yet all that becomes ancient history when we contemplate what his money has bequeathed not only to those who happen to live in New York, but to the millions of visitors from all over the world who have shared our pleasure and will continue to do so.

The same thing could be said for such other national legacies as the Chicago Institute of Art, the Field Museum in Chicago, the William Rockhill Nelson Museum in Kansas City, the Huntington Library in California, and many other such institutions across the country, not to mention the many buildings, research centers, scholarship programs and other benefactions which help keep the universities alive and functioning today.

What began as the gifts of rich individuals later became, in our time, the philanthropy of great corporations, carried out in a number of ways. Now, a new phase of business's contribution to the quality of life has begun to occur in a number of places, where the headquarters of the businesses themselves have become something more than skyscrapers. In several cities of the nation (it must be said that Canada and some European countries are already ahead of us in this respect) corporate buildings are designed to provide various kinds of amenities for the community itself in the form of arcades, plazas, parks and other means of enhancing the urban environment.

For example, we are about to have one of the best of these buildings in New York City, and from a kind of business noteworthy for such contributions in the past. In 1976, Citibank (once better known as First National City Bank) began construction of a new 46-story office building in midtown Manhattan. Its unique design represents a major assault on both urban blight and the kind of faceless architecture that has made empty, dangerous streets out of skyscraper-lined thoroughfares at night.

This building also represents a unique extension of retailing. The concept is embodied in the first three floors of the building, which comprise a skylit atrium, surrounded by approximately 30 specialty shops, cafés, food markets, restaurants, and shops which will carry related food items such as cookbooks, cooking utensils, and housewares from all over the world. The specialty food shops will be international in character. They will include both restaurants and take-out services for those who want to bring the products of their favorite foreign cuisine into garden and fountain areas in the center and eat in landscaped surroundings at tables provided for their convenience. For those who want to take their food home, there will be specially prepared packaging.

This international marketplace, which may be called "The Market," covers about 60,000 square feet, and can be entered from four different streets. The shops on three levels will ring the atrium, with its tables and umbrellas and fountains, and its cafés in shrubbed, flowery gardens, surrounded by fountains, walkways, and common seating areas.

I see this kind of development as an extremely hopeful sign for cities striving to maintain the vitality of their main business areas. While it is certainly not business philanthropy in any customary sense, and no one pretends that it is a non-profit enterprise, it is on the other hand a use of corporate money which, like museums, will bring pleasure not only to New Yorkers but to millions of tourists. It should also mean profits for the 30 or so small businessmen who will be operating the shops.

It's easy to see how ventures of this kind, multiplied by the hundreds, perhaps the thousands, will do much to make urban centers more meaningful than they have ever been for the people who live and work in them. They may not mean much to the potential small businessmen to whom this book is addressed, preoccupied as they are with getting started, making a living and holding a business together in a difficult world. But to me "The Market," together with the more traditional kinds of philanthropy, corporate and personal, represent what business should ultimately be about—that is, not the simple making of money by one formula or another, but the making of money to enrich human life beyond the struggle for existence. If that makes me an idealist and a utopian, so be it, but it is what I have learned from my life in retailing, and an ideal I hope to help realize.

Distributors

GIFTWARE DEALERS

AMERICAN CUT CRYSTAL CORP.
225 Fifth Ave.
New York, N. Y.
212-685-5850

ANCHOR HOCKING CORP.
415 Madison Ave.
New York, N. Y.
212-TE 8-9300

BROCKWAY GLASS CORP.
277 Park Ave.
New York, N. Y.
212-826-5000

J. G. DURAND INTERNATIONAL
225 Fifth Ave.
New York, N. Y.
212-532-8640

FEDERAL GLASS CO.
280 Park Ave.
New York, N. Y.
212-986-9705

WHEATON PRODUCTS
225 Fifth Ave.
New York, N. Y.
212-532-1833

CRYSTAL CLEAR, INC.
235 E. 53 Street
New York, N. Y.
212-753-3078

JEANNETTE CORP.
41 Madison Ave.
New York, N. Y.
212-532-9181

LIBBEY GLASS
405 Lexington Ave.
New York, N. Y.
212-692-8000

NIKKO CERAMICS, INC.
220 Fifth Ave.
New York, N. Y.
212-889-2590

THE SENDAR CO.
127 Fourth Ave.
New York, N. Y.
212-477-4200

BERNARD LIPMAN CO., INC.
225 Fifth Ave.
New York, N. Y.
212-689-1950

DAVAR PRODUCTS, INC.
15 W. 26 Street
New York, N. Y.
212-MU 3-0866

ALFRED KNOBLER & CO.
225 Fifth Ave.
New York, N. Y.
212-OR 9-5577

INTERNATIONAL SOLGO, INC.
77 W. 23 Street
New York, N. Y.
212-OR 5-3555

HARUTA & CO., INC.
137 Fifth Ave.
New York, N. Y.
212-677-9685

MIKASA
20 Enterprise Ave.
Secaucus, N. J.
212-279-7025

NORITAKE CO., INC.
41 Madison Ave.
New York, N. Y.
212-481-3300

LAUGHLIN HOMER CHINA CO.
225 Fifth Ave.
New York, N. Y.
212-MU 3-0619

KASUKA SALES, LTD.
212 Fifth Ave.
New York, N. Y.
212-LE 2-2840

PITMAN-DREITZER, INC.
1115 Broadway
New York, N. Y.
212-WA 4-7700

ARNART IMPORTS, INC.
212 Fifth Ave.
New York, N. Y.
212-683-7400

ROBINSON KNIFE CO.
1150 Broadway
New York, N. Y.
212-MU 3-3495

LIPPER INTERNATIONAL
225 Fifth Ave.
New York, N. Y.
212-686-6076

SEYMOUR MANN IMPORTS
225 Fifth Ave.
New York, N. Y.
212-683-7262

MIDLAND ENTERPRISES, INC.
1115 Broadway
New York, N. Y.
212-675-8300

NATIONAL SILVER CO.
241 Fifth Ave.
New York, N. Y.
212-MU 9-7300

RAIMOND SILVER MFG. CO.
225 Fifth Ave.
New York, N. Y.
212-889-5277

STYSON, INC.
543 W. 23 Street
New York, N. Y.
212-CH 2-3210

TOSCANY IMPORTS, LTD.
245 Fifth Ave.
New York, N. Y.
212-583-8740

SCIO POTTERY CO.
220 Fifth Ave.
New York, N. Y.
212-MU 9-1740

ONEIDA, LTD.
99 Park Ave.
New York, N. Y.
212-OX 7-1410

LIBERTY DISTRIBUTORS, INC.
110 W. Graham Ave.
Hempstead, N. Y.
516-895-1090

STANLEY ROBERTS
230 Fifth Ave.
New York, N. Y.
212-889-4250

REGENT-SHEFFIELD, LTD.
70 Schmitt Blvd.
Farmingdale, N. Y.
516-293-8200

HOUSEWARE DEALERS

GOTHAM INDUSTRIES, INC.
1150 Broadway
New York, N. Y.
212-683-2186

REGAL WARE, INC.
200 Fifth Ave.
New York, N. Y.
212-WA 4-6066

HUTZLER MFG. CO.
45-36 21 Street
Long Island City, N. Y.
212-ST 4-6288

WALL TRADING CORP.
182 Sweet Hollow Road
Old Bethpage, N. Y.
516-694-8660

MASBACH, INC.
330 Hudson Street
New York, N. Y.
212-AL 5-1300

EKCO HOUSEWARES CO.
230 Fifth Ave.
New York, N. Y.
212-532-4542

HUDSON-BERLIND CORP.
35 Engel Ave.
Hicksville, N. Y.
516-931-2800

ENTERPRISE ALUMINUM CO.
393 Seventh Ave.
New York, N. Y.
212-736-9050

JULIE POMERANTZ, INC.
230 Fifth Ave.
New York, N. Y.
212-MU 3-5670

S. FISHMAN CO., INC.
550 W. John Street
Hicksville, N. Y.
516-433-6800

PRETTY PRODUCTS, INC.
1115 Broadway
New York, N. Y.
212-WA 4-7700

GENERAL HOUSEWARES CORP.
101 Broad Street
Stamford, Conn.
212-421-3350

LIFETIME CUTLERY CORP.
241 41 Street
Brooklyn, N. Y.
212-499-9500

H. SCHULTZ & SONS
777 Lehigh Ave.
Union, N. J.
212-227-7325

LINCOLN METAL PRODUCTS CORP.
225 42 Street
Brooklyn, N. Y.
212-965-2887

LOROMAN CO., INC.
230 Fifth Ave.
New York, N. Y.
212-MU 3-2511

PEARL-WICK CORP.
1150 Broadway
New York, N. Y.
212-RA 1-3000

WASHINGTON FORGE, INC.
Harrison Ave.
Englishtown, N. J.
212-349-2227

WEAR-EVER ALUMINUM, INC.
270 North Ave.
New Rochelle, N. Y.
212-686-7910

SMALL APPLIANCES DEALERS

GRAYBAR ELECTRIC CO.
21-15 Bridge Plaza North
Long Island City, New York
212-EX 2-2000

HAMILTON BEACH
Division of Scovill Mfg. Co.
733 Third Ave.
New York, N. Y.
212-OX 7-3222

HANKSCRAFT MOTORS, INC.
369 Lexington Ave.
New York, N. Y.
212-TN 7-1870

KNAPP-MONARCH CO.
60 E. 42 Street
New York, N. Y.
212-682-4262

LEEDS-FOX, INC.
State Highway #10
E. Hanover, N. J.
212-LO 4-9420

GENERAL ELECTRIC SUPPLY CO.
26-45 Brooklyn-Queens Expwy.
Woodside, New York
212-626-9010

PROCTOR SILEX CORP.
230 Park Ave.
New York, N. Y.
212-689-8760

SPRINGER MORTON
& CO., INC.
129 Market Street
Kenilworth, N. J.
201-241-9755

SUNBEAM CORP.
128 W. 31 Street
New York, N. Y.
212-244-1747

WEST BEND CO.
393 Seventh Avenue
New York, N. Y.
LW 4-1922

HORN BROS., INC.
751 Summa Avenue
Westbury, New York
212-895-5290

AMCO-McCLEAN CORP.
766 McLean Avenue
Yonkers, N. Y.
914-BE 7-4000

FARBERWARE ELECTRICAL APPLIANCES
100 Electra Lane
Yonkers, N. Y.
914-237-8800

McGRAW-EDISON CO.
192 Lexington Ave.
New York, N. Y.
212-689-6900

COLLEGIATE SALES CORP.
175 Clearbrook Road
Elmsford, N. Y.
914-592-3774

I. LEHRHOFF & CO.
560 Belmont Avenue
Newark, N. J.
212-962-9036

NEGIN-FLETCHER, LTD
1 Pennsylvania Plaza
New York, N. Y.
212-594-2465

COSMETICS DEALERS

CHESEBROUGH-POND'S, INC.
33 Benedict Place
Greenwich, Conn.
203-661-2000

FABERGE, INC.
1345 Avenue of Americas
New York, N. Y.
212-581-3500

HELENA RUBINSTEIN, INC.
300 Park Ave.
New York, N. Y.
212-751-9100

LANVIN-CHARLES OF THE RITZ, INC.
40 W. 57 Street
New York, N. Y.
212-489-4500

REVLON, INC.
767 Fifth Ave.
New York, N. Y.
212-758-5000

MAX FACTOR & CO.
40 W. 57 Street
New York, N. Y.
212-489-9590

PRINCE
MATCHABELLI
33 Benedict Place
Greenwich, Conn.
203-661-2032

ELECTRONICS DEALERS

ARVIN INDUSTRIES
235 E. 31 Street
New York, N. Y.
212-MU 5-6866

ZENITH RADIO CORP.
666 Fifth Ave.
New York, N. Y.
212-CI 5-1400

EMERSON RADIO CO.
51 W. 51 Street
New York, N. Y.
212-765-9694

OLYMPIC INTERNATIONAL LTD.
8989 Union Turnpike
Glendale, N. Y.
212-261-9300

PILOT RADIO CORP.
66 Field Point Road
Greenwich, Conn.
203-327-0156

RCA
30 Rockefeller Plaza
New York, N. Y.
212-CO 5-5900

SONY CORP.
47-47 Van Dam Street
Long Island City, N. Y.
212-361-8600

BRUNO-N.Y., INC.
460 W. 34 Street
New York, N. Y.
212-LO 4-1252

GENERAL ELECTRIC CO.
570 Lexington Ave.
New York, N. Y.
212-PL 1-1300

MITSUBISHI
INTERNATIONAL CORP.
277 Park Ave.
New York, N. Y.
212-922-6684

SYLVANIA ELECTRIC
PRODUCTS
730 Third Ave.
New York, N. Y.
212-551-1000

E. J. GREEN, INC.
200 Madison Ave.
New York, N. Y.
212-686-6100

HARDWARE DEALERS

AMALITE, INC.
13-15 131 Street
College Point, N. Y.
212-939-7750

BERNZ-O-MATIC CORP.
740 Driving Park Ave.
Rochester, N. Y.
201-WY 2-5820

WALTER HARDWARE
Amber & Hagert Streets
Philadelphia, Pa.
215-427-2700

COASTAL ABRASIVE
P. O. Box 337
Trumbull, Conn.
203-375-5955

BAUMRIN BROS.
303 W. 10 Street
New York, N. Y.
212-YU 9-7900

LAMAR HARDWARE
2480 Butler Place
Bronx, N. Y.
212-CY 9-0275

MELNARD MFG. CORP.
153 Linden Street
Passaic, N. J.
201-472-8888

GENERAL ELECTRIC CO.
95 Hathaway Street
Providence, R. I.
212-964-1722

DURALL TOOL CORP.
923 Old Nepperhan Ave.
Yonkers, N. Y.
914-YO 8-8888

EXACT LEVEL & TOOL MFG. CO.
High Bridge, N. J.
201-638-6131

GREAT NECK SAW MFG. CO.
165 E. Second Street
Mineola, N. Y.
516-746-5352

HANDI-MAN FASTENERS
191 Fabyan Place
Newark, N. J.
212-962-1414

CENTURY HARDWARE CO.
4601 Woolworth Ave.
Milwaukee, Wisc.
414-353-7670

RAACO CORP.
372 Ely Ave.
South Norwalk, Conn.
212-725-2112

SWINGLINE, INC.
3200 Skillman Ave.
Long Island City, N. Y.
212-EM 1-8555

STANDEL PRODUCTS
92 Taff Ave.
Hempstead, N. Y.
516-538-3420

STEELCRAFT TOOLS
885 Centennial Ave.
Piscataway, N. J.
201-885-1400

GRIES REPRODUCER CO.
125 Beechwood Ave.
New Rochelle, N. Y.
914-NE 3-8600

GENERAL ELECTRIC CO.
133 Boyd Street
Newark, N. J.
212-750-2182

DYMO PRODUCTS
10 Parsonage Road
Edison, N. J.
201-895-2333

HOWARD HARDWARE
38 Davey Street
Bloomfield, N. J.
201-748-8100

HOLD ALL MFG. CO.
3 Cross Street
Suffern, N. Y.
914-357-6688

OMEGA PRECISION
HAND TOOL, INC.
18-39 128 Street
College Point, N. Y.
212-359-3120

PLUTO TOOL CO.
68 North Central Ave.
Valley Stream, N. Y.
516-LO 1-2033

ROCKWELL INTERNATIONAL
175-25 Horace Harding Expwy.
Flushing, N. Y.
212-225-2040

HENRY C. SCHAERF CORP.
360 E. 72nd Street
New York, N. Y.
212-734-2700

MARCEL MIRROR CO.
Bldg. #127 - Brooklyn Navy Yard
Brooklyn, N. Y.
212-875-3093

MANTON CORK CORP.
28 Benson Lane
Merrick, N. Y.
516-868-5600

LUSTRA TILE, INC.   METALCO WALL TILE CO.
375 Executive Blvd.   258 Herricks Road
Elmsford, N. Y.   Mineola, N. Y.
914-592-5265   516-741-7960

AUTOMOTIVE DEALERS

REALFLEX PRODUCTS CO., INC.   THERM-X OIL CO.
54 Knickerbocker Ave.   74 Mall Drive
Brooklyn, N. Y.   Commack, N. Y.
212-497-1777   516-334-6969

SAL METAL PRODUCTS CO., INC.   DANAL INDUSTRIES
120 Freeman Street   212 Fifth Ave.
Brooklyn, N. Y.   New York, N. Y.
212-389-2560   212-686-6355

WALLFRIN INDUSTRIES   INTERDYNAMICS, INC.
1535 Hart Place   78 18 Street
Brooklyn, N. Y. 11224   Brooklyn, N. Y.
212-373-7000   212-499-0608

ALBERT BLOCH & SONS, INC.   YANKEE METAL
444 Bayview Ave.   PRODUCTS CO.
Inwood, N. Y.   25 Grand Street
212-471-9500   Norwalk, Conn.
                                     212-PL 1-7270

ORIGINAL AUTO PARTS CORP.
195 West First Street   PYLON MANUFACTURERS
Mt. Vernon, N. Y.   Cross & Oak Streets
914-OW 9-9660   South Amboy, N. J.
                                     201-721-2295

RAPID AUTO SUPPLY, INC.
3535 Lawson Blvd.   QUAKER STATE OIL
Oceanside, N. Y.   Box 989
516-536-8330   Oil City, Pa.
                                     814-676-1811

BROADWAY MFG. CO.
E. State & High Streets   UNION CARBIDE CORP.
Camden, N. J.   270 Park Ave.
609-966-5330   New York, N. Y.
                                     212-551-2615

RUSKIN SPONGE
Commerce Drive & Enterprise Road   BURGESS INDUSTRIES
Montgomery, Pa.   Franklin Turnpike
215-368-6161   Saddle Brook, N. J.
                                     201-444-7350

ALLISON CORP.
200 Soth Ave.
Garwood, N. J.
201-789-2020

LEE FILTER DIVISION
191 Talmadge Road
Edison, N. J.
201-487-8400

HEALTH AND BEAUTY AID DEALERS

L. S. AMSTER CO.
190 Broadway
New Hyde Park, N. Y.
212-895-3545

MEAD-JOHNSON LABS
3605 Park Ave.
South Plainfield, N. J.
212-242-3940

KETCHUM DISTRIBUTORS, INC.
909 Remsen Ave.
Brooklyn, N. Y.
212-649-9500

S-P DRUG CO.
100 Apollo Street
Brooklyn, N. Y.
212-388-0800

LEDERLE LABS
Midtown Road
Pearl River, N. Y.
212-LO 2-7000

McKESSON & ROBBINS
DRUG CO.
90-30 Metropolitan Ave.
Rego Park, N. Y.
212-830-4500

PAUL LEDERMAN, INC.
125 Louis Street
South Hackensack, N. J.
201-440-1600

PHOTOGRAPHY DEALERS

IMC DIVISION OF
INTERPHOTO CORP.
220 Clay Ave.
Lyndhurst, N. J.
212-279-8444

MINOLTA CORP.
101 Williams Drive
Ramsey, N. J.
201-825-4000

ITT
133 Terminal Road
Clark, N. J.
212-239-8980

KEYSTONE CORP.
474 Getty Ave.
Clifton, N. J.
201-546-2800

SERVICE MFG. CO.
155 Saw Mill River Road
Yonkers, N. Y.
914-476-1700

GTE SYLVANIA, INC.
1000 Huyler Street
Teterboro, N. J.
212-CH 4-8820

UNIPHOT, INC.
61-10 34 Ave.
Woodside, N. Y.
212-779-5700

COMPASS INSTRUMENT CO.
104 E. 25 Street
New York, N. Y.
212-GR 3-2614

ACME LITE CO.
4650 W. Fulton Street
Chicago, Ill.
312-379-6860

BAIA CORP.
9353 Leerd
Jackson, Mich.
517-522-8461

DALITE CORP.
Route 15 North
Warsaw, Ind.
215-HI 9-4568

POLAROID CORP.
95 West Century Road
Paramus, N. J.
201-265-6900

EASTMAN KODAK CO.
1334 York Ave.
New York, N. Y.
212-879-1500

GAF CORP.
140 W. 51 Street
New York, N. Y.
212-582-7600

BELL & HOWELL CORP.
200 Smith Street
Farmingdale, N. Y.
516-293-4030

DEJUR AMSCO CORP.
45-01 Northern Blvd.
Long Island City, N. Y.
212-361-8200

DURACELL PRODUCTS
Berkshire Blvd.
Bethel, Conn.
203-792-2222

HOLSON CO.
111 Danbury Road
Wilton, Conn.
203-762-8661

IDEAL TRADING CO.
1123 Broadway
New York, N. Y.
212-YU 9-0980

RECORD AND TAPE DEALERS

MCA DISTRIBUTING CORP.
445 Park Avenue
New York, N. Y.
212-759-7500

ACB RECORDS
56-16 37 Avenue
Woodside, N. Y.
212-476-0500

NEW MUSIC DISTRIBUTION
6 West 95 Street
New York, N. Y.
212-749-6265

CANDY STRIPE RECORDS, INC.
17 Alabama Avenue
Island Park, N. Y.
212-895-2693

ALPHA DISTRIBUTING CORP.
20 West End Avenue
New York, N. Y.
212-586-6200

BETA RECORD DISTRIBUTORS, INC.
599 Tenth Avenue
New York, N. Y.
212-239-0440

CAPITOL RECORDS
1370 Avenue of Americas
New York, N. Y.
212-757-7470

CAYTRONICS CORP.
240 Madison Avenue
New York, N. Y.
212-889-0044

COLUMBIA RECORD SALES
45-20 83 Street
Elmhurst, N. Y.
212-898-1900

LONDON RECORD DISTRIBUTING
541 West 25 Street
New York, N. Y.
212-255-8350

MALVERNE DISTRIBUTORS, INC.
35-35 35 Street
Long Island City, N. Y.
212-392-5700

POLKA TOWN MUSIC
211 Post Avenue
Westbury, N. Y.
516-334-6228

SUTTON DISTRIBUTORS, INC.
960 East Hazelwood Avenue
Rahway, N. J.
201-382-7770

PETERS INTERNATIONAL, INC.
619 West 54 Street
New York, N. Y.
212-977-5600

RCA RECORDS
1133 Avenue of Americas
New York, N. Y.
212-598-5900

RECORDED AUDITORY MATERIALS, INC.
170-21 Jamaica Avenue
Jamaica, N. Y.
212-765-2585

RECORD PEOPLE
66 Greene Street
New York, N. Y.
212-226-7388

SMG DISTRIBUTORS, INC.
46-50 54 Avenue
Maspeth, N. Y.
212-937-7200

WARNER/ELEKTRA/ ATLANTIC CORP.
75 Rockefeller Plaza
New York, N. Y.
212-484-8580

MR. TOPP TAPE CO., INC.
239 Sunrise Highway
Rockville Centre, N. Y.
516-764-2512

APEX-MARTIN RECORD SALES
467 Mundet Place
Hillside, N. J.
201-923-7474

SURPLUS RECORDS & TAPES
68 West Passaic Street
Rochelle Park, N. J.
201-843-2670

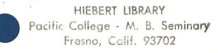